THE CALIFORNIA WINE COUNTRY HERBS AND SPICES COOKBOOK

COMPILED AND EDITED
by
Robert & Virginia Hoffman

© 1994. The California Wine Country Herbs and Spices Cookbook. All rights reserved. This book, or any portion thereof, may not be reproduced in any form, except for review purposes, without the written permission of The Hoffman Press, P.O. Box 2996, Santa Rosa, CA 95405-0996.

Printed in the United States of America

ISBN # 0-9629927-5-5

Typesetting and proofreading by
Nancy LaMothe, Sebastopol, Ca.

Printing by Griffin Printing Co.
Sacramento, Ca.

The Cover: "Golden Vineyard Hills of California"
by Ellie Marshall, Santa Rosa

Illustrations of herbs and spices courtesy of American Spice Trade Association. Drawings from "The Spice Cookbook," by A. Day and L. Stuckey. © 1964, 1991. All rights reserved. Published by David White Company, Willsboro, NY 12996. Used with permission.

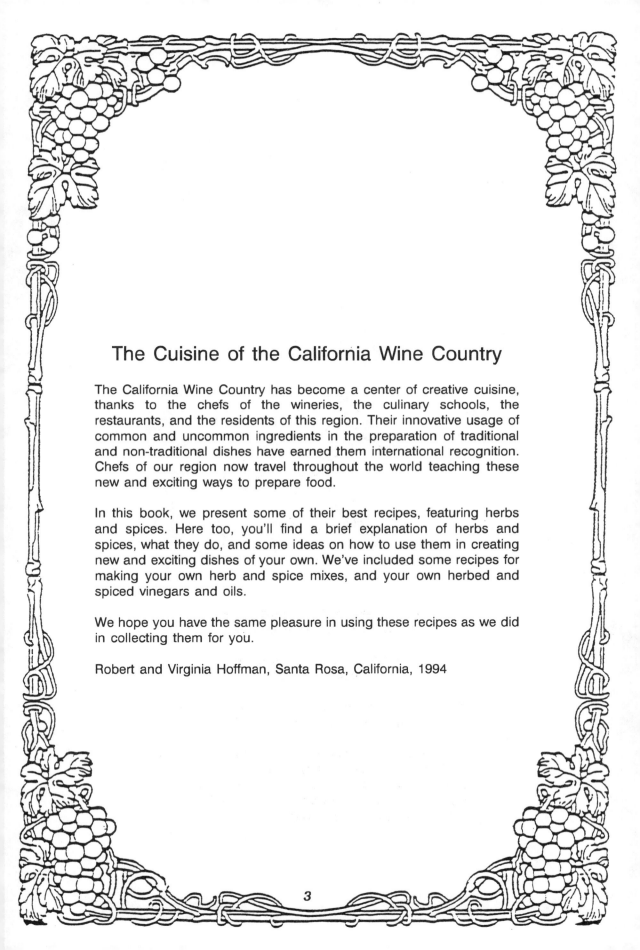

The Cuisine of the California Wine Country

The California Wine Country has become a center of creative cuisine, thanks to the chefs of the wineries, the culinary schools, the restaurants, and the residents of this region. Their innovative usage of common and uncommon ingredients in the preparation of traditional and non-traditional dishes have earned them international recognition. Chefs of our region now travel throughout the world teaching these new and exciting ways to prepare food.

In this book, we present some of their best recipes, featuring herbs and spices. Here too, you'll find a brief explanation of herbs and spices, what they do, and some ideas on how to use them in creating new and exciting dishes of your own. We've included some recipes for making your own herb and spice mixes, and your own herbed and spiced vinegars and oils.

We hope you have the same pleasure in using these recipes as we did in collecting them for you.

Robert and Virginia Hoffman, Santa Rosa, California, 1994

Table of Contents

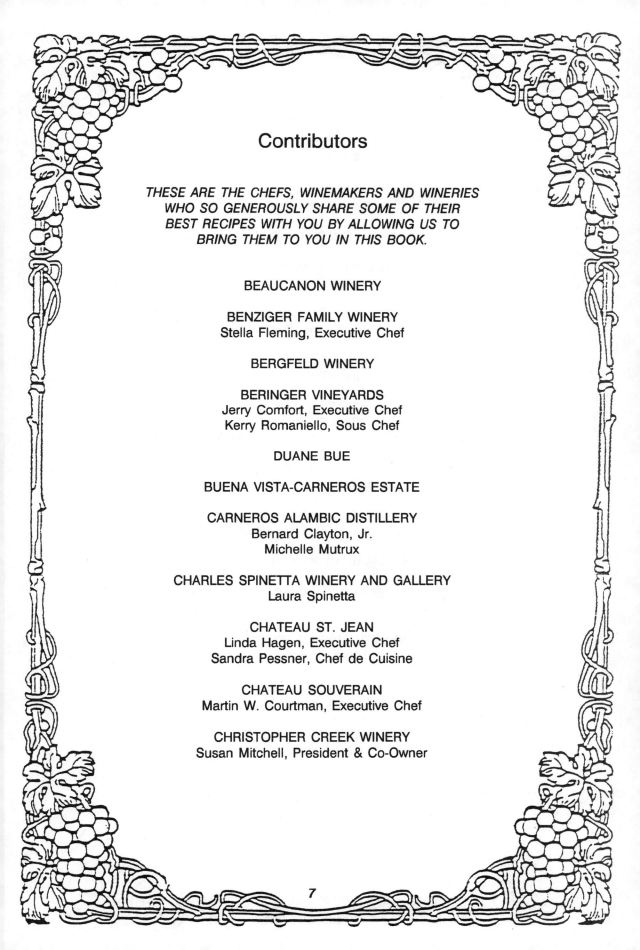

Contributors

THESE ARE THE CHEFS, WINEMAKERS AND WINERIES WHO SO GENEROUSLY SHARE SOME OF THEIR BEST RECIPES WITH YOU BY ALLOWING US TO BRING THEM TO YOU IN THIS BOOK.

BEAUCANON WINERY

BENZIGER FAMILY WINERY
Stella Fleming, Executive Chef

BERGFELD WINERY

BERINGER VINEYARDS
Jerry Comfort, Executive Chef
Kerry Romaniello, Sous Chef

DUANE BUE

BUENA VISTA-CARNEROS ESTATE

CARNEROS ALAMBIC DISTILLERY
Bernard Clayton, Jr.
Michelle Mutrux

CHARLES SPINETTA WINERY AND GALLERY
Laura Spinetta

CHATEAU ST. JEAN
Linda Hagen, Executive Chef
Sandra Pessner, Chef de Cuisine

CHATEAU SOUVERAIN
Martin W. Courtman, Executive Chef

CHRISTOPHER CREEK WINERY
Susan Mitchell, President & Co-Owner

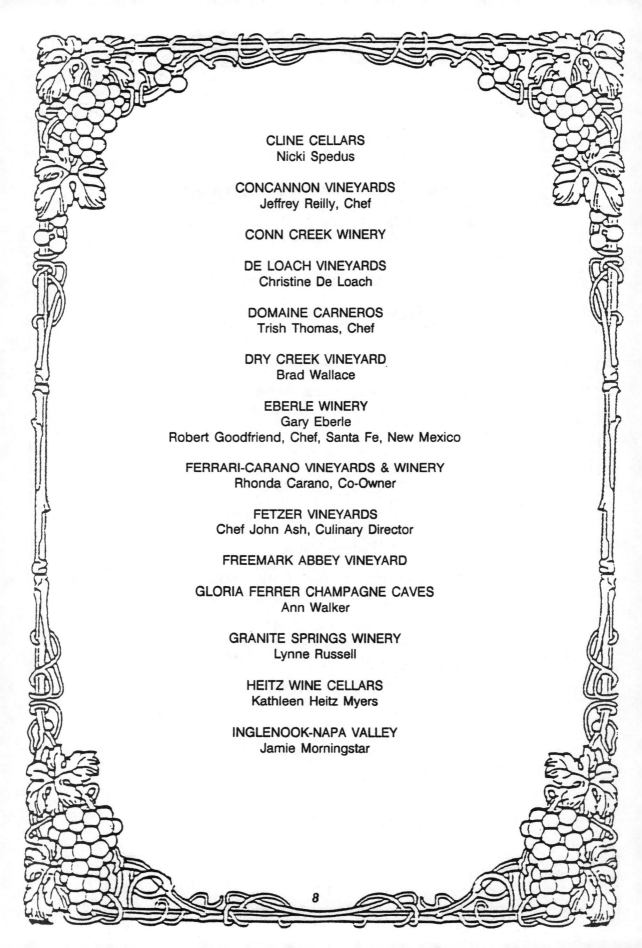

CLINE CELLARS
Nicki Spedus

CONCANNON VINEYARDS
Jeffrey Reilly, Chef

CONN CREEK WINERY

DE LOACH VINEYARDS
Christine De Loach

DOMAINE CARNEROS
Trish Thomas, Chef

DRY CREEK VINEYARD
Brad Wallace

EBERLE WINERY
Gary Eberle
Robert Goodfriend, Chef, Santa Fe, New Mexico

FERRARI-CARANO VINEYARDS & WINERY
Rhonda Carano, Co-Owner

FETZER VINEYARDS
Chef John Ash, Culinary Director

FREEMARK ABBEY VINEYARD

GLORIA FERRER CHAMPAGNE CAVES
Ann Walker

GRANITE SPRINGS WINERY
Lynne Russell

HEITZ WINE CELLARS
Kathleen Heitz Myers

INGLENOOK-NAPA VALLEY
Jamie Morningstar

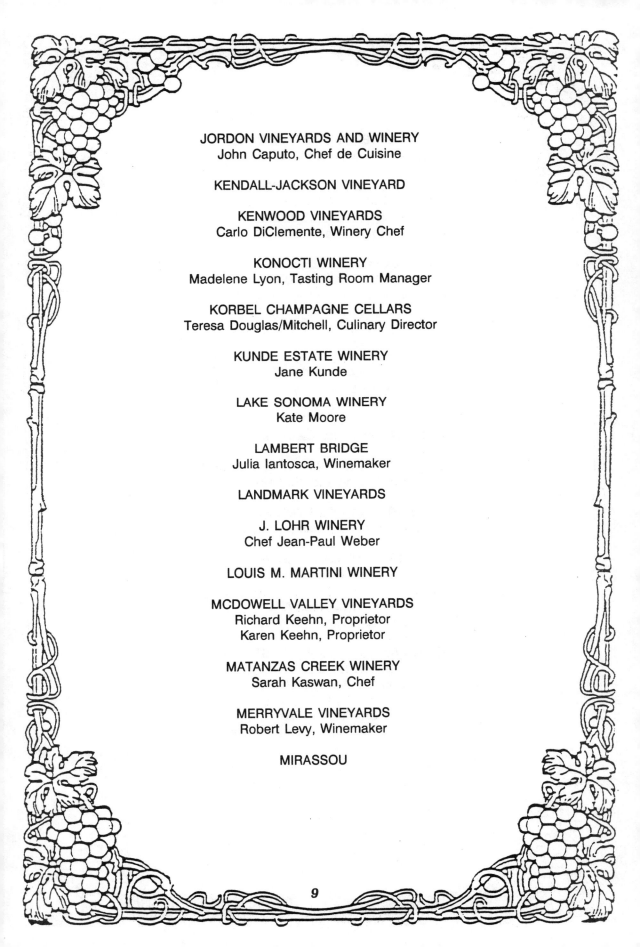

JORDON VINEYARDS AND WINERY
John Caputo, Chef de Cuisine

KENDALL-JACKSON VINEYARD

KENWOOD VINEYARDS
Carlo DiClemente, Winery Chef

KONOCTI WINERY
Madelene Lyon, Tasting Room Manager

KORBEL CHAMPAGNE CELLARS
Teresa Douglas/Mitchell, Culinary Director

KUNDE ESTATE WINERY
Jane Kunde

LAKE SONOMA WINERY
Kate Moore

LAMBERT BRIDGE
Julia Iantosca, Winemaker

LANDMARK VINEYARDS

J. LOHR WINERY
Chef Jean-Paul Weber

LOUIS M. MARTINI WINERY

MCDOWELL VALLEY VINEYARDS
Richard Keehn, Proprietor
Karen Keehn, Proprietor

MATANZAS CREEK WINERY
Sarah Kaswan, Chef

MERRYVALE VINEYARDS
Robert Levy, Winemaker

MIRASSOU

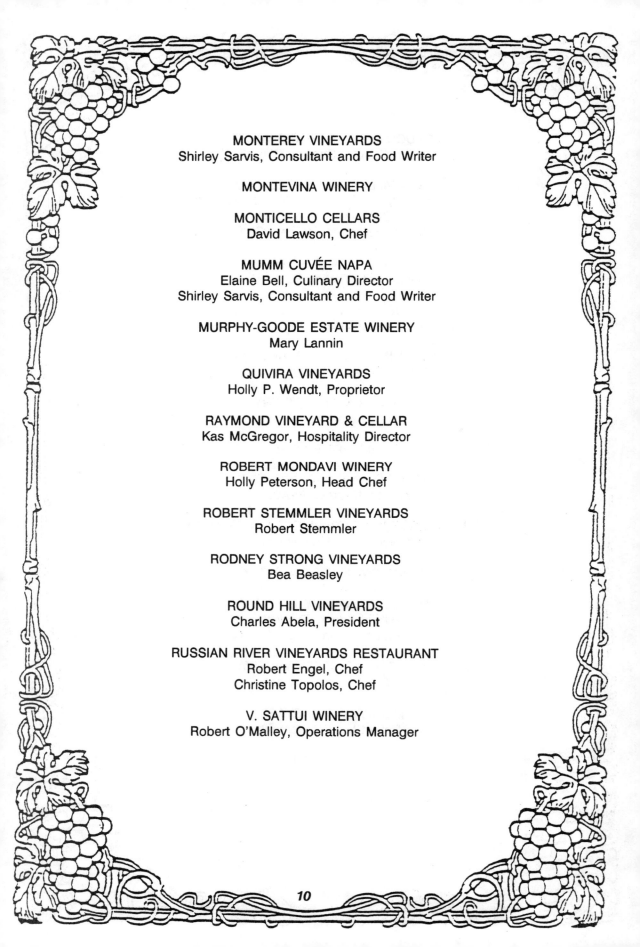

MONTEREY VINEYARDS
Shirley Sarvis, Consultant and Food Writer

MONTEVINA WINERY

MONTICELLO CELLARS
David Lawson, Chef

MUMM CUVÉE NAPA
Elaine Bell, Culinary Director
Shirley Sarvis, Consultant and Food Writer

MURPHY-GOODE ESTATE WINERY
Mary Lannin

QUIVIRA VINEYARDS
Holly P. Wendt, Proprietor

RAYMOND VINEYARD & CELLAR
Kas McGregor, Hospitality Director

ROBERT MONDAVI WINERY
Holly Peterson, Head Chef

ROBERT STEMMLER VINEYARDS
Robert Stemmler

RODNEY STRONG VINEYARDS
Bea Beasley

ROUND HILL VINEYARDS
Charles Abela, President

RUSSIAN RIVER VINEYARDS RESTAURANT
Robert Engel, Chef
Christine Topolos, Chef

V. SATTUI WINERY
Robert O'Malley, Operations Manager

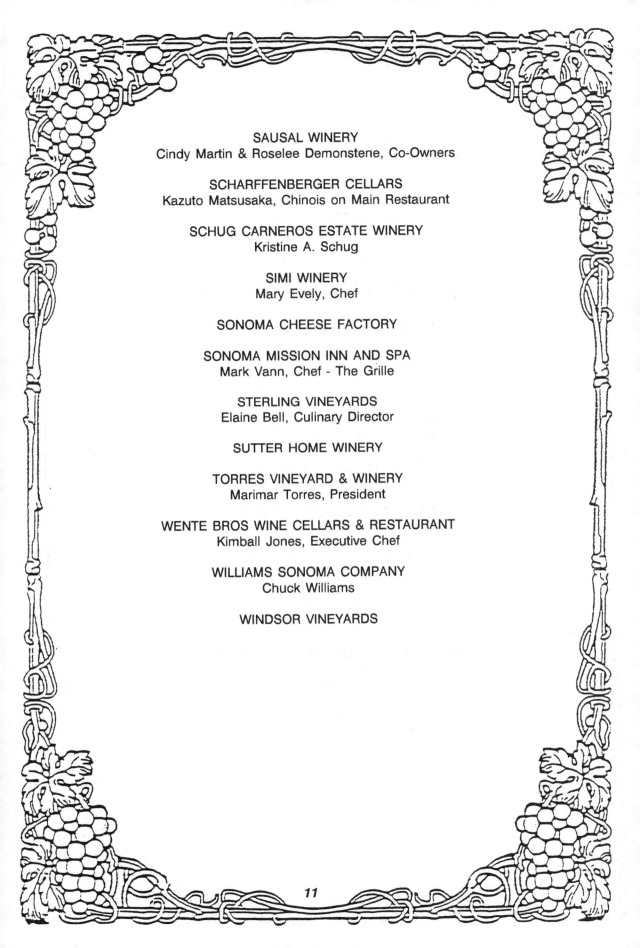

SAUSAL WINERY
Cindy Martin & Roselee Demonstene, Co-Owners

SCHARFFENBERGER CELLARS
Kazuto Matsusaka, Chinois on Main Restaurant

SCHUG CARNEROS ESTATE WINERY
Kristine A. Schug

SIMI WINERY
Mary Evely, Chef

SONOMA CHEESE FACTORY

SONOMA MISSION INN AND SPA
Mark Vann, Chef - The Grille

STERLING VINEYARDS
Elaine Bell, Culinary Director

SUTTER HOME WINERY

TORRES VINEYARD & WINERY
Marimar Torres, President

WENTE BROS WINE CELLARS & RESTAURANT
Kimball Jones, Executive Chef

WILLIAMS SONOMA COMPANY
Chuck Williams

WINDSOR VINEYARDS

Herbs and Spices...
What They Are and What They Do

ALLSPICE
A native of the Caribbean, it got its name because its aroma suggests a blend of cloves, nutmeg, and cinnamon. Available both whole and ground. Use the whole berries in meat broths, gravies and pickling liquids. Use the ground in fruit pies, preserves, relishes and with yellow vegetables. Try it, too, in chowder and bouillabaisse, and when steaming fresh fish.

ANISE
A medicine in ancient Assyria, and a charm against bad dreams and "the evil eye" in olden times, anise has a pleasant licorice flavor. Customarily used in making breads and rolls, on fresh fruit, and in mild cheeses. Use it to enhance the flavor of roast poultry, beef stew, and fricasseed veal.

BASIL
Originally from India, Hindus plant it around their homes and temples to insure happiness. Romantic Italians wear a sprig of basil as a sign of being in love, and in France it is called the herbe royale, as its aroma is highly esteemed. Here, we use this aromatic, anise-like herb with, or in place of, oregano. Commonly used in pastas, pizza sauces, and for macaroni and cheese casseroles. To add real dimension to most cooked green vegetables, add a pinch of basil.

BAY LEAVES

An old saying, "To win a laurel wreath for your brow, put a laurel leaf in the stew pot now," refers to the basil leaf, which is really the leaf of the laurel tree. It has a fragrant, aromatic odor, with a slightly bitter taste. Beef stew, chicken pot pies, and oxtail and pepperpot soups are naturals for bay leaves. An important ingredient in garni. Use it sparingly -- one or two leaves are enough.

CARAWAY SEEDS

Roman soldiers, two thousand years ago, brought caraway seed to Europe and England. They used the oil, ground it to make flour and considered it an essential part of their rations. Sold whole, with excellent keeping qualities, it has a warm, slightly sharp taste. In Germany it is used in making bread and pie crusts, and for flavoring pork, cabbage, sauerkraut, and beef stew. In Austria it is boiled to make a broth. In Italy it is boiled with peanuts.

Here in the California Wine Country it is used in marinades for lamb, veal, and beef roasts, in coleslaw, potato salad, and cottage cheese, and to make cheese spreads. Note: To maximize flavor, lightly crush the seeds.

CARDAMOM

This second most precious spice from India was discovered by the Vikings in their travels, which is probably why, to this day, all baked goods in Scandinavia seem to have this spice in them. Such diverse foods as coffee cake, sweet pickles, French dressing and frankfurters call for cardamom. It is also used in the Middle East in making coffee. In India it is the essential element in curry-making. Cardamom is the key ingredient of "Old Bay Seasoning," a blend of herbs and spices, used in making chowders, gumbos, and seafood ragouts.

CAYENNE & CHILI PEPPER

Also known as Red Pepper, it is another spice of the Americas, originating in the Caribbean. First noted in the annals of Christopher Columbus, the historian, Peter Martyr, who accompanied him on his voyages, said "There are innumerable kinds of peppers more pungent than that from Caucasus" (referring to the traditional pepper from Asia).

Cayenne and chili peppers are not pepper, but species of chilies called capsicum, with varying degrees of hot peppery flavor. Both are available in leaf and ground form. Cayenne is the hottest of the chili peppers, and is used to add authority to chili con carne, barbecue sauces, and similar foods of Latin America. Chili powder is usually a blend of various chilies to produce a smooth, yet warming flavor, without the harshness of cayenne. Like cayenne it is used in a wide variety of foods. Add baked fish, swiss steak plus a dusting on tomato and mushroom soups to the list of dishes to try with these "peppers".

CELERY FLAKES

Not a true herb or spice, this dehydrated essence of celery has a sweet, strong typical celery odor and taste. Add it to soups, stuffings or stewed tomatoes, and to garnish potato salad or meat sauces.

CELERY SEED

The name is a misnomer. It is actually the seed of the smallage plant, a distant wild relative of celery. It has a warm, slightly bitter celery odor and taste. Beef stew, meat loaf, dill, sweet, and mixed vegetable pickles, tamale pie, swiss steak, sloppy Joes, barbecue chili, chicken, oysters, vegetable soups, and French dressing are just some of the foods that are enhanced by this versatile spice. Garnish cole slaw, potato salad, and salad dressings, too.

15

CHIVES

It was not until the freeze drying process made this member of the onion family readily accessible throughout the year and throughout the United States, that it has become such an important element in American cuisine. Chives have unlimited uses in cooking. Add chives to all cooked green vegetables and green salads. Cheese and egg dishes, cream sauces, gravies, soups, and casseroles get a nice lift from chives. Garnish cottage cheese, sour cream, too.

CINNAMON

According to Chinese mythology, the Cinnamon tree was in the Garden of Paradise when the earth was born, and eternal happiness was granted to all who partook of it. In Greece it has been used for centuries in making stew; in India for making curries; in Europe for baking breads and pastries.

Here, in the California Wine Country, chefs use cinnamon in a wide variety of dishes with great results. Some of these are: Cous Cous, lamb stew, chicken casseroles, on mashed yams, and on baked plantains.

CLOVES

The clove forests of Indonesia spawned some of the bitterest wars for many years in Europe and between Europeans and the islanders who grew them, for the demand in Europe was intense for this strong, sweet, pungent tasting spice.

Besides studding a baked ham with the whole cloves, ground cloves are an important ingredient in making baked beans, chili, steak sauces, French dressing, and is essential in making good split pea soup. Try ground cloves when you poach fish, or make a beef stew.

CORIANDER SEED
Used by man since prehistoric times, coriander seeds have been found in Egyptian tombs of 960 B.C. It is described in the Old Testament of the Bible as well. You may be more familiar with the leaves of this plant, called "cilantro," or "Chinese parsley."

It has a distinctive mild lemon-like taste, but is really not appreciated in most kitchens, and it should be. You'll enjoy what it does in making curried chicken, a rice pilaf and broiled lamb.

CUMIN SEED
This is another spice that predates Biblical times. Many superstitions have clung to cumin. It was the symbol of the miser, and a happy life awaited the bride and groom who carried it at their wedding ceremony. Strong, aromatic, and somewhat bitter, it is known best as an ingredient in chili con carne, taco sauce, tamale pie, enchiladas and Spanish rice. It will add zest to fettucini primavera, bean soup and to brown rice.

DILL SEED/WEED
Once thought to "hinder witches of their will," dill has also been used as a medicine and as a nerve-calming tea. Both are usually available in the whole form. It has a clean, aromatic odor, with a warm caraway-like taste. Use the seed to make dill pickles, pickled beans and beets, of course. But also use it in potato salad, sauerkraut, and with vegetables such as cauliflower, broccoli, and green beans. Potent. Use 1/4 teaspoon for four to six portions.

The dill weed, which is slightly milder, is a natural for poached, broiled or baked fish, as well as sauces for any seafood.

FENNEL SEED
Its warm, sweet, anise-like odor and taste made it a very popular ingredient in Italian bread making and in making pasta sauces for centuries, but does not reflect on its colorful history of being believed to be an aphrodisiac, an aid to weight loss, and to sharpen eye sight. Try it in making seafood salad, beef stew and in pasta and bean soups

GARLIC

It was not until shortly after the end of World War II that garlic became an important element in cooking in the United States, although it has been a staple since Biblical times. The United States learned about garlic when American soldiers, returning from service in Europe, introduced it here. This interest in garlic was expanded when we were introduced to Chinese, Korean, Thai, and Cambodian cuisines in the past thirty years, all of which rely upon garlic as an important ingredient in their cooking.

Try garlic powder in mashed potatoes, a dusting on steamed vegetables, and just before you serve tomato, onion, split pea, or navy bean soup, add a very little bit of garlic powder.

GINGER

Gingerbread, the first known use of ginger, goes back to 2400 BC, and is credited to Greece as the first nation to use it to flavor foods. Soon adopted by the Romans, then in Europe, it was a wealthy person's delicacy for many centuries.

The root of a lily-like plant, it is washed, dried and sold fresh and in powder form. It can be found in virtually every produce department, in the fresh root form, and, of course, in every line of spices in the powder form. An important ingredient in Chinese cuisine, it is equally versatile in other cuisines as well. Try fresh ginger -- a piece one inch by one inch, shredded, in a pot roast, and on roast chicken or turkey. Also use ground ginger on carrots, and sweet potatoes, dust some on baked squash, and best of all, make gingerbread!

MACE

If you think of mace as a strongly flavored nutmeg, you'll have guessed its secret -- it is part of the nutmeg fruit. The nutmeg is made from the seed, the mace is the flesh of the fruit that is dried in small pieces and ground to a powder. Mace is a key ingredient in making ketchup, steak sauce, baked beans, frankfurters, bologna, and spreads of ham, chicken, and liver.

You may enjoy its distinctive flavor in making clam chowder, oyster stew, split pea and chicken soups. But be careful because it is potent. Try a very little bit (1/16 of a teaspoon) in making soup for six or eight, for example.

MARJORAM

In ancient times marjoram was considered the herb of happiness. Wreaths of it were worn by a bride and groom, and it was used to ward off the evils of witchcraft. A member of the mint family and distantly related to oregano, this herb is a valuable asset in the kitchen. Wonderful in meat stews, in poultry stuffing, and in the making of split pea soup, it is equally good in vegetable salad dressings, seafood sauces, and on roasted new potatoes.

MINT

The traditional mint julep of Kentucky has its origin in ancient Greek mythology when mint was a symbol of hospitality. Best known for its use with lamb, it has many other uses as well. Here in the California Wine Country we use mint, not only in mint sauce, but in making mint vinegars, chocolate desserts, and adding a touch of mint to new potatoes, peas and carrots, and to mushroom dishes.

MUSTARD

Literature of the medieval period of England abounds in mentions of mustard accompanying mounds of ham served to the gentry. While mustard is still primarily used with meat, it may also be used to make wonderful sauces for salmon and other saltwater fish, in making potatoes au gratin, in cheese sauces, and in vinaigrette dressings. For something innovative, make a mustard sauce to serve with green beans or asparagus.

NUTMEG

If you have ever smelled or tasted fresh ground nutmeg, you will appreciate the position that nutmeg enjoys in the hierarchy of spices. So versatile in its usages, it is an essential component in many cakes, cookies, pastries and puddings, while it enjoys a similar position in flavoring meats, vegetables, pastas and even fruit. Available in both whole and ground form, it is worth the extra effort to use the whole and grind it freshly for every use. Try nutmeg in chicken soup, making herbed butter, and in candied sweet potatoes.

ONION
Purists say that the onion is not a member of either the herb or spice categories, but is a vegetable. Anything that does as much to enhance and flavor foods, in addition to its own attributes as a vegetable, deserves honorable mention here. Available dried in flakes, minced, and as onion salt. (Warning: Onion salt is salt mixed with dehydrated onion. Don't use in salt-restricted diets.)

OREGANO
In the United States, oregano owes its fame to pizza, and pizza owes its status in this country to the armed forces who, returning from Italy after World War II, raved about the "tomato pies" they had there. In less than ten years pizza and oregano had become household words and chefs were finding new uses for this savory herb. In addition to its usage in pizza and pasta sauces, it is rubbed into roasting meats, laid on charcoal embers to flavor grilled foods, stuffed into large baked fish, and used in making beef, chicken and vegetable broths.

PAPRIKA
The slightly sweet mild odor and taste of paprika make it hard to believe that it is a member of the capsicum family, which produces chili peppers. But the flavor is only part of its accomplishments, as it imparts a rich reddish color to the foods in which it is used. Often used simply to garnish such foods as baked potatoes, cottage cheese, etc., it is an important flavor ingredient, too, in the preparation of stews, goulash, and chili con carne. A word of caution; keep it out of sunlight. When it fades, this delicate spice's flavor fades, too.

PARSLEY
Parsley is best known as the principal ingredient in French cuisine via its presence in bouquet garni and aux fines herbes, the former being finely chopped parsley mixed into dishes such as quiche, and the latter being the little bag of herbs and spices suspended into the cooking dish and removed prior to serving. Its mild flavor goes well with poultry, fish, and egg dishes. Use it as a garnish in salad dressing, casserole dishes, cottage cheese and soups. You may choose to use a sprig to decorate your plate. Particularly useful as a breath freshener, too!

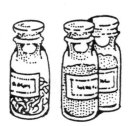

PEPPER

Like salt, pepper is one of oldest seasonings known to man. Both black pepper and white pepper come from the berries of the same vine. Black pepper is harvested before the berry is fully ripe. White pepper allows the berry to ripen fully making it easy to remove the black husk, leaving the white berry. Both are available in whole, medium and coarse ground. It would be impossible to list all the foods that lend themselves to the use of pepper, both black and white. Do remember, however, that black pepper is more pungent than the white, but white pepper is far hotter. If a recipe calls for "pepper" chances are nine out of ten times, it is calling for black pepper. Most recipe writers specify white, when it is desired.

POPPY SEEDS

The mature seed of the poppy comes from the same plant that produces opium, but because the seed is formed after the plant has lost its opium production capability, there is no narcotic effect in poppy seeds. So tiny that it takes 900,000 to make a pound, they add completely new flavors with poppy seed butter (just brown the poppy seeds in butter until they turn golden), as a sauce on noodles, rice, new potatoes, boiled onions, broiled fish, and on nearly any cooked vegetable.

ROSEMARY

Best known for its delicate fragrance, immortalized in Shakespeare's Hamlet by Ophelia "There's rosemary, that's for remembrance," and used since time immemorial as the wreath for brides, it has a fresh bittersweet taste that goes well with lamb, chicken, and seafood. Use it sparingly, it can dominate a dish!

SAFFRON

Saffron, the world's costliest spice, is also one of the most potent in that only a few strands will flavor and color large quantities of a dish. Essential in the making of paella, the Spanish dish of rice, seafood, poultry and sausage; and also in Moroccan cous cous, the savory blend of lamb, semolina wheat, chick peas, onions, carrots, turnips, raisins, zucchini, eggplant and turnips. If you prefer to start with something simpler, use just two or three strands in boiling water when cooking rice, which will produce four to six portions of a rich, golden rice with a delicate, exotic flavor.

SAGE

Ancient herbalists believed that sage improved the memory and insured long life. Since colonial times in America, it has been considered an essential seasoning, particularly for split-pea soup, poultry stuffings, pork dishes, salad dressing and chowders.

Available in whole, ground, or "rubbed" form. (Rubbed sage is fluffy and imparts better flavor.) Make your own croutons for salads and soups by dusting sage on cubed bread before toasting.

SAVORY

There are two savories: Summer and Winter. The Summer is the milder of the two and the more useful, as it does not tend to dominate a dish as does the Winter variety. Use it for chicken pot pies, herbed rice, and, for something quite different, in creamed onions.

SESAME SEED

The Egyptians, 4,000 years ago, used sesame for its oil, as a grain and as a seasoning. We in the U.S. are indebted to the slaves who brought sesame from Africa as a reminder of their homeland.

This nut-like seed is sold untoasted, and may be used as an ingredient or a topping that will be baked or browned. But if you are going to use them as an ingredient, you must toast them first for 20 to 25 minutes in a baking dish in a medium oven. Stir until they are light brown and nutty flavored. You'll enjoy these toasted sesame seeds on hamburgers, sprinkled over any salad, on green beans instead of almonds, and as sesame butter to serve with fresh water fish.

TARRAGON

Its sweet, aromatic anise-like taste and odor make one think of the tropics, but unlike most herbs and spices that are from the tropical and temperate zones, tarragon is from the steppes of Siberia. It is most popular in France where it is one of the four components of fines herbes (chervil, chives, parsley, and tarragon in equal amounts). Makes a wonderful wine vinegar. Use it to flavor mayonnaise, and in poultry and fish stuffings.

THYME

"You smell of thyme" was one of the finest compliments one ancient Greek could pay another. Thyme was the symbol of elegance. This herb came to America from France and Spain, and became one of our most prolific seasonings. Its warm, fragrant aromatic odor and pungent taste are best used in making such diverse dishes as sauerbraten, chicken pot pie, pizza and spaghetti sauces, wine vinegars, and in salad dressings. Thyme butter is delightful over creamed white onions, braised celery, asparagus, green beans, eggplant and tomatoes.

TURMERIC

A stranger to most American kitchens, turmeric is a little appreciated herb whose taste is somewhat peppery, but whose coloring attribute ranks it as the poor cousin of saffron. Like saffron it imbues a warm golden yellow color which is most appealing in making Spanish rice, curries, cheese spreads, and in making mustard sauces.

Herb and Spice Mixes

A great convenience is a selection of herb and spice mixes that are ready to use in the preparation of various foods. We are including some for you to use as they are ... and encourage you to make some variations or creations of your own.

Herb and spice mixes can also completely change the tastes of such stand-bys as meatloaf, stews, soups and roasts, making them exciting new dishes.

Herb and spice mixes are particularly helpful if diets are restricted to little or no salt. They can provide the necessary flavor without the use of salt.

VEGETABLE SOUP MIX
2 teaspoons dried basil
2 teaspoons celery seed
2 teaspoons dried chervil
2 teaspoons dried parsley
1 teaspoon dried rosemary
1 teaspoon dried sage
2 teaspoons dried thyme

THAI SPICE BLEND
1/8 teaspoon ground cinnamon
1 teaspoon ground coriander
1/2 teaspoon ground cumin
1/2 teaspoon garlic powder
1/2 teaspoon ground ginger
1/2 teaspoon onion powder
1/4 teaspoon ground red pepper

MEXICAN BLEND
1/2 teaspoon chili powder
1 teaspoon cilantro
1/2 teaspoon ground coriander
1 teaspoon ground cumin
1 teaspoon onion powder
1/2 teaspoon red pepper

MEDITERRANEAN BLEND
1 teaspoon ground coriander
1 teaspoon ground cumin
1 teaspoon garlic powder
1 teaspoon onion powder
1 teaspoon oregano leaves
1/4 teaspoon ground red pepper
1/2 teaspoon thyme leaves

CHILI POWDER (SALT-FREE)
6 dried hot chilies, 2 to 4 inches
1 1/2 teaspoons dried cumin seeds
2 teaspoons of dried oregano
1 teaspoon sweet paprika
1/2 teaspoon garlic powder (optional)

Grind all ingredients in spice mill until they are very fine. Makes about 1/3 cup.

CURRY POWDER
This is a basic recipe for a curry powder. We urge you to make just a little bit and try it (this recipe makes about four tablespoons). Then develop your own, by increasing and/or decreasing the elements of it. For example, if you want it milder, use less white pepper, red pepper and ground ginger. It you want it hotter, just increase them.

1 teaspoon ground allspice
4 teaspoons ground coriander
1 teaspoon cumin seeds
1 teaspoon fenugreek seeds
1/2 teaspoon ground ginger
1 teaspoon dry mustard

1/4 teaspoon red pepper
 flakes
1/2 teaspoon white peppercorns or ground white pepper
3 teaspoons ground turmeric

Grind and mix together thoroughly. Saute in a little butter or margarine over a low heat, for a minute or two to blend, and to release the flavors, before adding to other ingredients.

BEEF MIX
4 teaspoons black pepper, medium grind
2 teaspoons garlic powder
4 teaspoons onion powder
4 teaspoons dried parsley

SEAFOOD MIX
2 teaspoons dried basil
2 teaspoons dried chervil
2 teaspoons dried marjoram
1 teaspoon dried parsley
3 teaspoons dried tarragon

POULTRY MIX
2 teaspoons dried basil
2 teaspoons dried chervil
2 teaspoons dried parsley
2 teaspoons dried rosemary
1 teaspoon dried thyme

LAMB MIX
2 teaspoons dried parsley
4 teaspoons dried rosemary
3 teaspoons dried thyme
2 teaspoons garlic powder
   (optional)

Making Your Own
Herbed Vinegars and Oils

Herb vinegars and oils are very easy to make, require a few simple ingredients, take very little time to prepare, and will provide you with a bouquet of flavors that will turn ordinary, every-day dishes into something truly special.

Both the vinegars and the oils require the same methods of making, the same utensils, and, other than the choice of using oils or vinegars, the same herbs and spices.

UTENSILS:

A plastic funnel. A yard or two of cheesecloth or paper coffee filters. A stainless steel, glass, or granite pot, but not aluminum, to heat the ingredients for the heating method. Measuring spoons and cup.

You'll need a pint- or quart-size, wide mouthed glass jar for the Steeping Method.

Bottles: We suggest you use the standard 750 mm wine bottles or quart bottles, but you may proportion the recipes here to fit the size bottle you wish to use. New corks: You can get them at most hardware stores, or those stores that sell home winemaking and beer brewing supplies.

PREPARATION:

Place all your bottles in the bottom rack of your dishwasher upside down and wash and dry thoroughly. If you do not use a dishwasher, place the bottles in a pot of boiling water for five minutes and dry carefully to remove all moisture. Lightly cork the bottles.

FOR MAKING HERB AND SPICE VINEGARS:

There are seven kinds of vinegars: Red Wine, White Wine, Champagne, Cider, Malt, Rice, and White. The Red Wine, White Wine, Champagne, and Rice all make great herb vinegars. Don't use the Cider, Malt, or White as they are too strong and the herbs and spices do not blend well with them.

Here in the California Wine Country we prefer the three wine vinegars, and they are all readily available throughout the United States and Canada.

FOR MAKING HERBED AND SPICED OILS:

Corn, Olive, Safflower and Sunflower oils are all good (olive is the best, however). Be sure that the one you choose does not have a strong taste of its own.

HERBS AND SPICES:

You may use fresh, or dried whole, powdered or flaked herbs or spices in whatever form they are available where you live. The only difference you will find is that the dried, flaked and powdered herbs that you buy in a grocery store are somewhat stronger than the ones that you grow and dry yourself, and thus require lesser quantities.

STEEPING AND HEATING METHODS:

The differences between the two are that the Steeping Method requires steeping for one to three weeks, and the Heated Method produces a vinegar or oil that you can use immediately. Both methods are good, but the Cold Method will give you a better herbed vinegar or oil, particularly when you are using the more delicate or subtle herbs, such as cardamom seed, basil, thyme and parsley.

THE STEEPING METHOD:

1. Place the herbs in the amounts noted (see individual recipes which follow) in a sterilized steeping bottle. Pour the desired quantity of vinegar or oil into the bottle, covering the herbs completely. Cork the bottle and shake vigorously. Store for the noted period of time, shaking when you think of it, every few days.

Strain through a paper coffee filter or a doubled cheesecloth into your sterilized bottle. If you wish, place a fresh or dried sprig or leaves of the herb in the bottle for decor and added flavor. Cork it tightly with a new cork, and label it. You have it, ready to use.

THE HEATING METHOD:

Place the herbs in the amount noted (see individual recipes which follow) in a sterilized steeping bottle. Heat the vinegar or oil until it is bubbling, but not boiling, and pour into the bottle, covering the herbs. Cork the bottle and shake vigorously. Let it cool in the steeping bottle.

Strain through a paper coffee filter or a doubled cheesecloth into your sterilized bottle. You may want to place fresh or dried sprigs or leaves of the herb in the bottle. Cover it tightly with a new cork, and label it.

TOO STRONG OR TOO WEAK?

If it is too strong, dilute with the same vinegar or oil that you used. If it is too weak, replace herbs/and or spices with a fresh batch and repeat process.

NOW, ON TO THE RECIPES...

RECIPES:

We've standardized the recipes to use one pint of the selected vinegar or oil as the base measurement. If you are going to use pint bottles for your final bottling, use the base measurement of one pint (16 ounces/2 cups) for your recipe.

If you are using wine or champagne "splits" (375 ml) bottles, use 12 ounces (1 1/2 cups) of the selected vinegar or oil as your base.

If you are using standard wine bottles (750 ml) use 24 ounces (3 cups) of the selected vinegar or oil as your base.

Proportion your herb measurements accordingly.

BASIL VINEGAR:

1 pint champagne, red wine
  or white wine vinegar
6 fresh basil leaves
OR
1/2 ounce dried basil leaves

Place basil in steeping bottle, add hot (not boiling) vinegar, cork and shake. Let cool, strain after about two hours of steeping. This will produce a mild basil vinegar. For a more potent basil vinegar, let it steep for a week, then strain and cork.

Use in tomato dishes like pasta sauces, etc. Good with fish, poultry dishes and salad dressings.

31

CORIANDER VINEGAR:

1 pint white wine vinegar
2 ounces coriander seeds
OR
1 ounce coriander powder

Crack the coriander seeds by rolling pin or mortar, and place in steeping bottle with the vinegar. Steep in a warm place for two to three weeks. Strain, pour into bottle, cork and label.

This herbal vinegar will add great flavor to pan fried fish, sausages, frankfurters and hamburgers.

DILL SEED VINEGAR:

1 pint white wine vinegar
1 ounce dried dill seed
2 or 3 dill weed sprigs (optional)

Combine the vinegar with the dill seed in the steeping bottle, and let them steep for five to seven days. Strain and bottle. Add the optional dill weed sprig, if you wish.

Good for potato salads, pasta salads, coleslaw and salad dressings.

DILL WEED VINEGAR:

1 pint white wine vinegar
6 spring or branches fresh dill,
 without seeds
OR
1/2 ounce dried dill,
 without seeds

Place the sprigs of dill in the steeping jar with the vinegar and let it infuse for two weeks. Strain and put into your bottle, with one or two sprigs of the dill. Cork and label.

Dill weed vinegar is quite different from dill seed vinegar. It is quite mild in comparison. Use it for salads, soups and seafood.

FENNEL VINEGAR:

Fennel vinegar is made the same way that dill weed vinegar is made.

Please note that fennel is unusual in the family of herbs and spices in that it tastes like licorice, but it does not impart this taste to other foods. Rather, it enhances the flavor of the foods with which it is used. Try it on cooked vegetables.

GARLIC VINEGAR:

1 pint red wine or white wine vinegar
4 cloves fresh, peeled garlic, bruised
  and coarsely chopped
OR
1 ounce garlic powder or flakes
Pinch of salt (optional)

Place garlic in steeping bottle, add the vinegar, cork and let it steep for two weeks. Shake it once or twice as week. After two weeks, strain and bottle.

Use it for salads and marinades with caution. Garlic becomes quite powerful when used in this form.

ROSEMARY VINEGAR:

1 pint champagne or white wine vinegar
6 fresh rosemary leaves
OR
1 ounce dried rosemary

Place leaves, then vinegar into steeping bottle, and shake vigorously. Let stand for five to seven days, shaking it daily, if possible. Add a whole leaf or a sprig for trim if you wish.

Great for beef, lamb and pot roast basting. Try it to add zest to boiled new potatoes and cauliflower when steaming or boiling.

TARRAGON VINEGAR:

1 pint champagne, or white wine vinegar
1 ounce fresh tarragon leaves
OR
1/2 ounce dried tarragon leaves

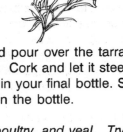

Heat the vinegar to bubbling, <u>not boiling</u>, and pour over the tarragon, which you have placed in the steeping bottle. Cork and let it steep for five to six days, or a week. Strain and place in your final bottle. Some sprigs or leaves of tarragon may be placed in the bottle.

Use for salad dressings, green salads, fish, poultry, and veal. Try it in sauces and in egg dishes.

CLOVE & CINNAMON OIL:

2 cups vegetable oil
8 whole cloves
2 sticks of cinnamon

Warm the oil on low heat for five minutes. Place cloves and cinnamon in bottle, and pour oil in bottle slowly. Cork and put aside for two weeks.

For sauteing beef and in a beef stew. Also ideal for oiling cake pans and scrambling eggs.

GARLICKY HERB OIL:

1 cup light vegetable oil
1 cup virgin olive oil
1 clove of garlic, bruised
1 large or 2 small sprigs of fresh tarragon
1 large or 2 small sprigs of fresh rosemary
3 or 4 juniper berries (optional)

Wash the fresh herbs and dry thoroughly. Mix the two oils together in a pan and heat on low heat for five minutes. Place all other ingredients in bottle, and fill the bottle with the warm oil. Cork tightly and keep two weeks before using.

Before broiling steak or pork chops, brush lightly with this oil, and repeat when meat is turned.

LEMON CHILI PEPPER OIL:

2 cups virgin olive oil
Peel of one lemon in one long,
  narrow strip if possible.
Your choice of any two red
  chili peppers, fresh or dried.

Place lemon, peppers and oil in steeping bottle, cover with cheesecloth, place in sunny spot, and stir every day or so.

Ideal for green salads, broiling chicken, and fish.

SPICY OIL:

2 cups light vegetable oil
3 whole cloves
3 whole allspice berries
2 cinnamon sticks
1 tablespoon coriander seeds
6 cardamom pods, crushed
10 whole black peppercorns
Peel of half a lemon

Warm the oil in a pan over low heat for five minutes, remove from stove, and add all ingredients. Stir gently, and put into bottle. Cork tightly and wait two weeks before using.

This oil is ideal for salads, over pasta, and to brown any meat.

Appetizers
and
Light Foods

SPICES OF THE WORLD

Seared Venison Tartar with Pink Peppercorn Crust and Pickled Beets

8 ounces venison, ground through meat grinder on 1/4-inch die

2 tablespoons sundried cherries, diced

1 tablespoon raspberry vinegar

Salt and pepper

2-3 ounces of arugula with 1 beet, boil in rice wine vinegar, peel and julienne

1 loaf Olive Bread, cut into slices, brushed with olive oil and baked 10 minutes at 400 degrees

4 tablespoons pink peppercorns, crushed with rolling pin

Reserved beet vinegar mixed with olive oil and salt

Combine venison with sundried cherries, raspberry vinegar, salt and pepper; gently form into 2-ounce patties.

Press onto crushed peppercorns. Sear to order, on the side with peppercorns only, in saute pan.

PRESENTATION:

Arrange arugula in circle on plate and place patty in middle. Garnish with 2 croutons and sprinkle with julienne beet. Drizzle with beet vinaigrette. Serves 4.

Wine Suggestion: Beringer Gamay Beaujolais.

Jerry Comfort, Executive Chef
Beringer Vineyards

A native Californian, Jerry Comfort has been with some of the most highly respected restaurants in California. He began as the chef at Eppaminondas Restaurant, then sous chef at Fourneau's Ovens at the Stanford Court, leaving there to help open Masa's Restaurant, then to work with Jeremiah Tower at Stars and the Santa Fe Bar & Grill.

His next project was as chef de cuisine at Domaine Chandon, followed by serving as executive chef at the award winning Checkers in Los Angeles. The lure of the Napa Valley was overpowering, and in 1991 he became executive chef of Beringer Vineyards.

Cheddar-Herb Scones

2 cups unbleached flour
4 teaspoons baking powder
1/2 teaspoon baking soda
1/2 teaspoon salt
1/2 cup chilled, unsalted butter,
 cut in small pieces
1 egg

3 tablespoons chopped fresh
 herbs like dill, basil, rosemary
 or chives
2/3 cup whipping cream
1/2 cup grated sharp cheddar
 cheese
Additional cream

Preheat oven to 400 degrees. Stir together flour, baking powder, baking soda and salt. Cut in the butter pieces until mixture resembles coarse meal. In a separate bowl, whisk together the egg, herbs, whipping cream and cheese. Add to the dry ingredients and stir just to combine.

Turn dough onto a lightly floured board and knead about ten times. Roll out into a 1/2-inch thick rectangle and fold in half. Roll out a bit more to about 3/4 inch thick. Cut out rounds with a floured cookie cutter. Brush tops of scones with additional cream and bake until golden, about 12 to 15 minutes.   Makes approximately 12 scones.

Serve with Benziger Family Sonoma County Chardonnay.

Stella Fleming, Executive Chef
Benziger Family Winery

Wild Mushroom Tarts
Canapé or Luncheon Entrée

TART PASTRY:

2 cups flour
1/2 teaspoon salt
1/2 pound butter, chilled

2 egg yolks
4 tablespoons ice water

WILD MUSHROOM FILLING:

5-6 shallots, minced
5 tablespoons butter
1/2 cup Champagne
1/2 pound domestic mushrooms,
minced
1/2 pound wild mushrooms,
minced

2 tablespoons brandy
1 3/4 cups heavy cream
1/4 cup mushroom liquid,
reduced
4 eggs, beaten
1/4 teaspoon cayenne pepper
Salt/white pepper to taste

In a food processor, combine the flour and salt. Pulse briefly to sift. Add the butter, one tablespoon at a time, and process until crumbly. Add the ice water and continue processing until dough just begins to form a ball. (Do not overprocess or the dough will be tough.) Wrap in wax paper and refrigerate, approximately 2 hours. Remove from the refrigerator and press into tart pans.

In a small pan over medium heat, melt 2 tablespoons butter. Add the champagne. Saute the shallots until all liquid is gone. Remove shallots and set aside.

In a medium pan over medium heat, melt 3 tablespoons butter. Add the brandy. Saute the mushrooms until tender. Using a slotted spoon, remove the mushrooms and set aside. Reduce the liquid to 1/4 cup.

In a medium bowl, whisk together the cream, eggs and cayenne pepper. Whisk in the mushroom broth and season to taste with salt and white pepper.

Evenly spread the mushrooms and shallots in the tart shells. Pour in the custard. Bake at 375 degrees for 20 to 30 minutes, until set. Makes 4 to 6 4-inch tarts.

Serve with Korbel Champagne/Blanc de Blancs.

Teresa Douglas/Mitchell, Culinary Director
Korbel Champagne Cellars

Cilantro Cured Salmon Tostada *

1 cup dried small white beans
1 piece, 1-inch cube, salt pork
 (optional)
2 fresh jalapeno peppers
4 ounces fresh goat cheese
6 large or 12 small white corn
 tortillas
Corn oil
1 bunch cilantro

1/4 pound cured salmon,
 sliced thin*
1 cup light sour cream
1/2 each red and yellow sweet
 peppers and red onion,
 chopped
A few drops of olive oil and
 rice wine vinegar

Soak and cook white beans according to package directions. Cut jalapeno peppers in half and remove seeds. Add, with optional salt pork, to the beans at the start of cooking. When tender, drain and remove pork and peppers, and let cool. Combine beans and goat cheese in food processor and puree.

Heat about 1 inch of corn oil in a heavy iron skillet and fry the tortillas just until they begin to color. Drain well on paper towels. Wash and de-stem cilantro. Combine sweet peppers and red onion, and moisten with a few drops of olive oil and rice wine vinegar.

To assemble, spread a little of the bean puree on each tortilla. Top with a handful of cilantro leaves and a slice of cured salmon. Spoon a little sour cream on, and sprinkle chopped peppers and onion over.

Serves 6.

* See Cilantro-Cured Salmon recipe, Page 140.

Serve with Simi Sauvignon Blanc wine.

Mary Evely, Chef
Simi Winery

Mary Evely says "I was raised in the Midwest on the traditional diet of overcooked meats, overcooked vegetables and Coke". A move to New York and then to Los Angeles started her on the path that led to her present position of Executive Chef of Simi Winery.

Now celebrating her tenth year at Simi, she has been a guest chef in France, and many prestigious restaurants throughout the United States. Her busy schedule includes lectures on food and wine pairing to wine societies, restaurants and the food and wine events at the winery.

Herbed Quesadillas

1/2 red onion, peeled and cut in 3/4-inch slices
2 tablespoons vegetable oil
8 8-inch flour tortillas
1 red bell pepper, roasted, peeled and cut into 1/2-inch strips
1/2 pound low-fat mozzarella cheese, grated

2 garlic cloves, peeled and minced
2 tablespoons fresh marjoram (or 1 teaspoon dried)
2 tablespoons fresh oregano (or 1 teaspoon dried)
Pinch of freshly ground black pepper

Preheat a grill or broiler. Brush the onion slices with 1 tablespoon of the oil and grill or broil 6 inches from the heat for 4 minutes on each side.

Heat a skillet over high heat. Soften the tortillas by grilling for 30 seconds on each side.

Mix the onion, red pepper strips, mozzarella, garlic, marjoram, oregano and pepper. Divide evenly over 4 tortillas and top with remaining 4, pressing them down gently. Brush both sides lightly with oil.

Preheat oven to 400 degrees. Bake the quesadillas for 3 to 5 minutes, or until lightly browned and the cheese is melted. Cut into quarters and serve immediately. Makes 16 pieces.

"These are one of my favorite party hors d'oeuvres since they are so easy and fast to make."

Wine Note: One of the richer California Chardonnays or Sauvignon Blancs will balance the texture and flavors of this recipe.

Carlo DiClemente, Winery Chef
Kenwood Vineyards

Oregano

Potato-Parsnip Pancakes with Smoked Salmon, Lemon Sour Cream and Fresh Dill

2 large russet potatoes
2 medium parsnips
2 egg whites
1/4 teaspoon ground nutmeg
Salt and freshly ground pepper
1/2 cup sweet unsalted butter
(melted)

12 ounces smoked salmon
1/2 cup sour cream
The zest of 1 lemon (chopped
very fine) plus 2 tablespoons
juice
4 large sprigs of fresh dill

PREPARING THE PANCAKES:

Preheat oven to 350 degrees. Peel potatoes and parsnips. Chop into small cube-size pieces that will fit in the feed tube of a food processor. Place the grating disk in your food processor and assemble the lid in place. Turn food processor on and put potato and parsnip cubes in feed tube. Press down through grating disk. To me, this is the easiest way to grate, but if you do not own a food processor, or you are not familiar with operating one, you may prefer to grate them with an old-fashioned grater.

Place grated potatoes and parsnips in a medium stainless steel bowl. In a separate bowl, beat the egg whites with a wire whisk. Add to the potatoes and parsnips. Add salt, pepper and nutmeg to potato-parsnip mixture. Combine well. Line a sheet pan with parchment paper. With a pastry brush, coat parchment paper with about 1/4 of the melted butter.

Take a small amount of potato-parsnip mixture into the palm of your hand and mold into a pancake shape. Keep in mind that you will either want to divide the mixture into 4 sections for 1 large pancake per person, or 8 sections for 2 small pancakes per person. Once you have molded the pancake, place onto buttered sheet pan. Repeat process with remaining mixture. Brush the tops of the pancakes with 1/2 of the remaining butter.

Put pancakes into preheated oven. Bake for 20 to 25 minutes or until golden brown and crisp on the bottom. Remove pan from oven and flip pancakes over with metal spatula. Brush tops again with remaining melted butter. Bake again for 20 minutes or until golden brown. Remove from oven and keep in a warm place.

TO ASSEMBLE THE DISH:

Start by adding the lemon zest and juice to the sour cream. Stir thoroughly. Slice the smoked salmon into 1 1/2-inch pieces. Place the pancakes in the center of each plate. Arrange the smoked salmon around the pancakes. Spoon the sour cream on top of each pancake and garnish with a sprig of dill.   Serves 4.

These pancakes are well worth the effort! They are baked slowly at a low temperature for the perfect texture from the potato and just the right sweetness from the parsnip. Once you try this recipe, you will love to make these pancakes for all occasions. They also go very well with homemade applesauce and sour cream.

Serve with a glass of Domaine Carneros Sparkling Wine.

Trish Thomas, Chef
Domaine Carneros

Trish Thomas, who is responsible for all of Domaine Carneros' culinary functions, was eleven years old when she made her first "Boule de Neige," for an appreciative commercial audience.

Her mother Linda Thomas, a nationally recognized caterer in the Napa Valley, recognized Trish's potential and, at an age when most children are playing with toys, Trish was at the stove and pastry board.

By fifteen, Trish was managing and baking for "The Croissant Place," a family enterprise. At the age of seventeen, she was catering major events, and by nineteen catered the prestigious Young President's Dinner at Robert Mondavi Winery.

Her current projects include the development of Domaine Carneros' culinary programs and her own epicurean education.

Dill

Savory Focaccia

1 tablespoon yeast	1/4 cup olive oil
2 cups all purpose flour	1/2 cup water
2 tablespoons salt	1/2 cup Chardonnay
3 tablespoons fresh basil, minced	1/4 cup crisp bacon, chopped
1 1/2 tablespoons fresh rosemary, minced	3 tablespoons minced onion, sauteed

Preheat oven to 450 degrees. Combine dry ingredients and herbs. Add olive oil, water, Chardonnay and remaining ingredients. Knead to form dough. Let rise. Punch down and set into a 14-inch, well oiled pan. Rise to double. Bake 10 to 15 minutes until golden.

Serving suggestions: Top with smoked salmon, sour cream and chives; or use as a crust for a white seafood pizza with you favorite shellfish and a mild cheese.

Serve with Beringer Vineyards 1990 Private Reserve Chardonnay.

Kerry Romaniello, Sous Chef
Beringer Vineyards

Green Olivado

1 10-ounce jar Spanish olives (green)	1 teaspoon oregano
1/4 cup blanched almonds	1 teaspoon thyme
2 teaspoons basil	1/4 cup olive oil

Drain olives, discard pimento and rinse well. Soak in cold water 10 minutes, then drain thoroughly. Place olives, almonds and herbs in a food processor. Whirl to chop and drizzle in olive oil while chopping. Makes 1 1/2 cups. Serve with crackers or Middle Eastern (pita) bread.

Serve with Lambert Bridge Sauvignon Blanc or Fumé.

Julia Iantosca, Winemaker
Lambert Bridge

Butternut Squash Pancake with
Baked Garlic Cream and Smoked Salmon

2-2 1/2 cups coarsely shredded
butternut squash
1 medium onion, coarsely chopped
4 tablespoons unsalted butter
1 teaspoon chopped fresh garlic
1/4 teaspoon ground mace
1/4 teaspoon marjoram
1/4 teaspoon thyme
1/4 teaspoon freshly ground
pepper
8-10 ounces smoked salmon

1 cup sifted all purpose flour
1 tablespoon sugar
1/2 teaspoon baking powder
1/2 teaspoon salt
3 large eggs, lightly beaten
1 cup milk
15-20 pieces thin, skinless
butternut squash, sauted in
butter till lightly brown,
season with sage, salt and
pepper

Saute onion and grated squash in 1 tablespoon butter for 3 to 5 minutes until lightly browned. Add garlic, mace, marjoram, thyme and pepper and saute 1 to 2 minutes more. Take off and cool.

Combine flour, sugar, baking powder and salt. Make a well in the center of the mixture. Put the eggs, milk and 3 tablespoons of melted butter into well. Stir just until moistened (will be lumpy). Stir in squash-onion mixture gently. Spoon out approximately 2-ounce portions onto preheated lightly oiled griddle or cast iron pan. Lay down 1 piece of sauted squash on each pancake and barely cover with a bit more batter. Turn when lightly brown. Let cool to room temperature.

BAKED GARLIC CREAM:

Bake 2 to 3 heads of garlic, wrapped in foil in 400 degree oven, for 40 to 50 minutes until soft. Squeeze out garlic and mash. Whip heavy cream to soft peaks and add garlic puree 1 to 2 teaspoons at a time, until nicely flavored. Season gently with salt and pepper.

To serve, place smoked salmon slice in rosette shape on top of pancake, fill center with garlic cream and garnish with 2 to 3 whole chive spears.   Serves 8.

Serve with Matanzas Creek Sonoma Valley Chardonnay.

Sarah Kaswan, Chef
Matanzas Creek Winery

Curried Chicken in Cracker Bread

2 Armenian cracker breads	1 teaspoon curry (or to taste)
4-6 chicken breasts (4 large or 6 small) poached and chopped	Salt and pepper
4 green onions, chopped	6 ounces cream cheese, softened with cream
Fresh parsley, chopped	1 small jar mango chutney
1/2 to 1 cup mayonnaise	1 cup peanuts, chopped
Lemon juice	1 bag alfalfa sprouts

Combine chicken, green onions and parsley. Blend mayonnaise, lemon juice, curry, salt and pepper. Mix well with chicken.

To soften cracker bread, quickly wet cracker bread under running water (30 seconds) and place between cotton towels for 1/2 hour to absorb excess moisture.

Spread cracker bread evenly with softened cream cheese, chutney, chicken mixture and sprinkle with peanuts and sprouts. Roll up tightly and chill 4 hours. Slice into 3/4 inch rolls.   Serves 8.

This dish is perfect for brunch, lunch or holiday parties. It is excellent accompanied by an off-dry, lightly fruity wine, such as Chateau St. Jean's Sonoma County Gewurztraminer.

Linda Hagen, Executive Chef
Chateau St. Jean

Zucchini Blossom Fritters with
Avocado Mousse and Smoked Tomato Sauce

2 baby zucchini with blossoms
 (per serving)
2 ounces smoked tomato sauce
Beignet Batter
1 small onion
1/4 cup olive oil

2 tablespoons lime juice
1 tablespoon basil
Salt and pepper
1 cup cream cheese
1 teaspoon cilantro
1/2 avocado

Remove zucchini blossoms. Cut zucchini into 1/8-inch thin slices. Blanch and chill. Finely dice onion. Combine zucchini, onion, olive oil and basil, season with salt and pepper.

Mix avocado with cream cheese, add lime juice and cilantro. Stuff each blossom with about 2 teaspoons of avocado/cream cheese mixture. Seal the top by pinching and twisting the open end gently.

Batter blossoms evenly in beignet batter (recipe follows) and deep fry until golden brown. Drain well on paper towels. Arrange zucchini vinaigrette around outside of plate; pour sauce (recipe follows) in center of plate. Place two fritters on sauce.

BEIGNET BATTER:
1/2 cup flour
1/2 cup cornstarch
1 tablespoon oil (preferably nut oil)
1 egg

2 teaspoons baking powder
Water
Salt and pepper

SMOKED TOMATO SAUCE:
6 Roma tomatoes, smoked and
 chopped
1/2 yellow onion, chopped

2 garlic cloves, chopped
2 teaspoons olive oil
Salt and pepper

Smoke roma tomatoes in smoker for approximately 6 minutes. Sweat onions in olive oil over low heat. Add chopped smoked tomatoes and garlic. Simmer for 30 minutes. Add salt and pepper. Puree and strain.

Wine Suggestion: Serve as first course with Beringer Fumé Blanc

Jerry Comfort, Executive Chef
Beringer Vineyards

Savory Stilton Cheese Tart

CRUST:

1 1/4 cups flour
1/4 cup Parmesan cheese, finely
grated
1/4 teaspoon salt

12 tablespoons butter (1 1/2
sticks)
1 egg yolk
3 tablespoons cold water

FILLING:

1 red onion, sliced
2 tablespoons butter
1/4 cup Blanc de Noirs
Champagne
1 1/2 cups heavy cream
6 egg yolks

1/4 teaspoon salt
1/8 teaspoon cayenne
1/8 teaspoon freshly grated
nutmeg (optional)
1/4 pound Stilton (or any blue
cheese), crumbled

To prepare the crust, place the dry ingredients in a food processor. Pulse to blend. Add the butter and run the machine until the mixture is crumbly. Pour in the egg yolk and water. Run the machine until a ball of dough is formed. Cover and chill for 30 minutes or so. Saute the onion in the butter. Moisten with the Champagne, and simmer until the liquid is absorbed. Set aside.

Whisk together the cream, eggs and seasoning for the filling. Roll out the tart dough and press it into a 10-inch pan. Crumble the cheese inside and spread the onions on top. Pour in the filling. Bake at 425 degrees for 10 minutes. Lower the temperature to 350 degrees and continue baking another 25 to 35 minutes (or until set).   Serves 8.

Serve with Korbel Champagne/Blanc de Noirs.

Teresa Douglas/Mitchell, Culinary Director
Korbel Champagne Cellars

Italian Gorgonzola Cheesecake

2 ounces Italian Gorgonzola
2 tablespoons unsalted butter,
 softened
2 ounces cream cheese, softened
3 eggs
2 1/2 tablespoons sour cream

1 1/2 tablespoons minced
 fresh basil
1/8 teaspoon salt
1/4 teaspoon white pepper
1/3 cup chopped walnuts

Heat oven to 350 degrees. Butter an 8-inch pie pan. With food processor, cream Gorgonzola with butter until very smooth. Add the cream cheese and blend. Add the eggs, one at a time, blending after each, until mixture is smooth. Add the sour cream, basil, salt and pepper, and mix well. Pour mixture into prepared pie pan and set the pie pan into a larger pan. Add enough hot water to come halfway up the side of the pie pan.

Bake in the oven until mixture is firm, golden and puffy, about 20 to 25 minutes. The last 5 minutes of cooking, sprinkle top with the chopped walnuts. Finish baking. Take out of oven to allow to cool. Pie will collapse. Cut into slim wedges and serve with sliced baguette French bread.   Serves 6 to 8.

May also add caramelized red onions on top for another option.

Serve with Ferrari-Carano Alexander Valley Cabernet Sauvignon.

Rhonda Carano, Co-Owner
Ferrari-Carano Vineyards and Winery

The Carano family divide their time between their home in the California Wine Country and their hotel and casino in Reno, Nevada, The Eldorado. It has achieved international recognition for the fine cuisine of its restaurants.

Basil

Roquefort Cheese Cheesecake

CHEESE FILLING:

8 ounces fresh ricotta cheese
8 ounces fresh goat cheese
8 ounces fresh cream cheese
5 ounces roquefort or gorgonzola
1/2 cup sour cream

1 whole egg
1/3 cup fresh basil or
 oregano, chopped
Lemon zest

CARAMELIZED ONION/APPLE LAYER:

2 small onions, thinly sliced
3 tablespoons butter
1 crisp apple, shredded
1 lemon, zest and juice

NUT CRUST:

1 cup walnuts/pecans, finely
 chopped
1/4 cup flour
1/4 cup butter, cold
3 tablespoons water, cold

CARAMELIZED ONION/APPLE PREPARATION:

Remove zest and juice from the lemon; peel onion and cut in half vertically. Lay flat and slice in thin, even slices. Over low heat, melt butter in a heavy saucepan, add onions and saute slowly to caramelize for 30 to 45 minutes, turning frequently (do not burn). Peel, core and shred crisp apple and toss with lemon juice. Set aside until onions are caramelized, then add to pan and saute for several minutes. (Save lemon zest for cheese filling.) While onions are cooking, prepare crust and cheese filling.

NUT CRUST PREPARATION:

Lightly grease a 10-inch flat bottomed spring-form pan (tin tends to discolor crust). Using a food processor, finely chop shelled nuts using ON/OFF button. Put 2 tablespoons nuts in the spring-form pan. Tilt and rotate to coat vertical sides of the pan, saving any loose nuts for garnish. Add flour and slices of cold butter to remaining nuts in processor turning ON/OFF to blend. Add water and again blend quickly until nut-dough is formed. Press a thin layer on the bottom of the pan. Set aside.

CHEESE FILLING PREPARATION:

Wash, dry and de-stem fresh herbs; finely chop in a food processor. Combine all ingredients (except roquefort) by using ON/OFF button to blend. Do not over process.

ASSEMBLY:

Preheat oven to 225 degrees. Spread caramelized onion/apple mixture on nut-crust bottom. Crumble roquefort on top of this mixture. Spoon cheese filling over top and spread evenly. Sprinkle remaining nuts on top. Fill a larger sided pan with 1 inch of hot water. Place the cheesecake in the center and bake in the water bath at 225 degrees for two hours or until set. This long, slow cooking insures a creamy texture. Remove from water bath and cool before sliding a clean knife around the edges to loosen. Remove side of spring-form pan. Allow one hour to set up before serving. Cut into wedge shaped pieces.
Serves 10 to 14.

Note: Take care to use dry, fresh onions and fresh, good quality cheeses that are not old or the combined flavors will be too strong to complement wine. This cheesecake can be covered with plastic wrap and refrigerated for several days. Use as an appetizer or light entree to take the place of a cheese course, or in place of dessert.

Karen Keehn, Proprietor
McDowell Valley Vineyards

Basil Pita Triangles with
Hummus and Red Pepper

3 tablespoons olive oil
1 teaspoon basil, chopped
1/2 teaspoon Kosher salt

5 whole wheat pita pockets
2 red bell peppers, roasted,
  peeled and julienned

Preheat oven to 450 degrees. Cut each pita into 8 wedges. Toss wedges with basil, salt and oil. Place evenly on baking sheets and bake for 4 minutes on each side.

Hummus

1 15-ounce can chickpeas with
liquid
1/4 cup lemon juice
1/2 cup Tahini (sesame paste)
1 tablespoon olive oil

1 clove garlic, minced
1/2 teaspoon cumin, ground
1/4 cup cilantro, reserve some
  leaves for garnish
Salt and pepper

Combine all ingredients in food processor and process until smooth. Adjust seasoning. Spread hummus on pita triangles. Crisscross strips of red bell pepper over the top and garnish with a cilantro leaf.

Yields 40 pieces.

Mark Vann, Chef - The Grille
Sonoma Mission Inn and Spa

Sweet
Pepper

Soups

SPICES OF THE WORLD

Brandied Peach and Plum Soup

2 cups each ripe peaches and plums, peeled, pitted and cut into chunks
1 1/2 cups water
1 1/2 cups dry white wine
2/3 cup sugar
1 slice lemon
1 cinnamon stick
3 tablespoons fine Brandy
Mint leaves, to garnish

Drop peaches into boiling-hot water for 5 seconds to loosen the skins. Slip off the skins, pit and cut into chunks. Wash plums, pit and cut into chunks.

Place the peaches, plums, water, wine, sugar, lemon and cinnamon in a medium (3-quart) saucepan. Bring to a boil, lower heat and simmer gently for about 20 minutes or until fruit is fork-tender. Allow mixture to cool somewhat so it can be comfortably worked through a chinois or sieve. Discard coarse pulp.

Set soup aside to cool. Add Brandy and adjust to taste. Add sugar and/or Brandy as needed. Chill for 3 hours or longer.

Serve in chilled cups and garnish with mint leaves, chopped fine.
Serves 4 to 5.

The soup may also be served hot. Try it first hot, then again after it has been chilled before deciding on your preference.

Bernard Clayton, Jr.
for
Carneros Alambic Distillery

Bernard Clayton, Jr., who created this recipe, is also the author of "The Complete Book of Soups and Stews."

Black Bean Chili

1 1/2 pounds dried black beans, picked over (3 1/2 cups)
1 tablespoon vegetable oil
2 large or 3 medium onions, chopped (2 cups)
6 large garlic cloves or more to taste, minced (2 tablespoons)
1 bay leaf
4 teaspoons cumin seeds or ground cumin
2 tablespoons sweet Hungarian paprika
1/2 teaspoon cayenne pepper
4 tablespoons chili powder
3 tablespoons dried oregano
1 large green bell pepper, seeded and diced

6-8 sundried tomatoes, chopped to make 1/3 cup
1 28-ounce can tomatoes, seeded and chopped with juice
1/4 cup bottled mild taco sauce
Salt to taste
1/2 teaspoon sugar
1 tablespoon cider vinegar
Freshly ground black pepper to taste
1/4 cup chopped fresh cilantro plus sprigs for garnish
6 tablespoons plain yogurt
6 tablespoons salsa

Soak beans overnight. Drain. Heat 1 teaspoon oil over medium heat in a large stockpot and saute 1 cup onions with 2 teaspoons garlic for 5 minutes, or until the onions begin to soften. Add beans, about 8 cups water, or enough to cover the beans by an inch, and bay leaf. Bring to a boil. Reduce heat to low, cover and simmer for 1 to 2 hours.

Meanwhile, toast cumin seeds in a dry heavy skillet over medium-high heat for 3 to 4 minutes, or until they begin to color. (If using ground cumin, heat until it is just beginning to smell fragrant and remove from the heat.) Shake the pan or stir the seeds constantly or they will burn. Remove from the heat, and add paprika and cayenne. Stir together for about 30 seconds in the hot pan. Grind the spices together in an electric spice mill or blender. Add chili powder and oregano.

In a second large casserole dish or stockpot, heat the remaining 2 teaspoons oil and saute the remaining 1 cup onions over medium-low heat until they soften, about 5 minutes. Add 2 teaspoons garlic and green peppers and continue to saute for about 5 minutes. Add spices and sundried tomatoes and continue sauteing, stirring constantly, for about 3 to 5 minutes, scraping the bottom of the pot carefully so that the spices don't burn. If they cake on the bottom of the pan, add a little water. Add tomatoes and their juice, about 1/2 teaspoon salt and sugar and bring to a simmer. Cover and simmer over low heat for 30 minutes, stirring often.

Add the beans with their liquid to the tomatoes and spices. Add the remaining 2 teaspoons garlic. Stir everything together and continue simmering, covered, for 2 hours or more until the beans are thoroughly tender and the broth is thick and fragrant. For a thicker chili, simmer, uncovered or partially covered, for the last half-hour of cooking. Remove bay leaf, stir in vinegar and pepper and adjust the seasonings, adding more chili powder, garlic, salt, pepper or a bit more vinegar, if desired. Stir in 1/4 cup cilantro just before serving.

To serve, ladle a generous portion of chili into each of six bowls and top with 1 tablespoon each of yogurt and salsa. Garnish with a few leaves of cilantro. Serves 6.

Serve with Granite Springs Petite Sirah or Zinfandel.

Lynne Russell
Granite Springs Winery

Corn Chowder

1 large white onion, diced
2 stalks celery, diced
2 carrots, peeled and diced
6 ears of fresh corn, removed from the cobs
3 cups chicken stock
1 cup cream
2 tablespoons chopped fresh thyme
2 tablespoons chopped fresh basil
3 strips of smoked bacon, diced
3/4 cup white wine
3 tablespoons corn oil
2 cloves minced garlic
Tabasco
Salt and pepper

Saute onions, carrots and bacon with corn oil until soft.

Add garlic and cook approximately 1 minute. Add white wine and cook 3 minutes over medium heat. Add corn, chicken stock, cream and thyme. Cook until tender. Add basil, salt, pepper and tabasco to taste. Remove 1/3 of the soup, puree in processor or blender and add back to remainder of the soup. Serves 6.

Serve with Concannon Vineyard Sauvignon Blanc

Chef Jeffrey Reilly,
of the Danville Hotel Restaurant & Saloon
for
Concannon Vineyards

Mary's Tortilla Soup

10 corn tortillas, torn in small pieces
10 cups chicken stock
4 boneless chicken breasts
1 large red bell pepper, diced
1 (or more) jalapeno, finely diced
1 red onion, diced

3 cloves garlic, finely minced
1 tablespoon cumin
1 tablespoon chili powder
1 tablespoon Worcestershire sauce
4 ounces tomato puree
Oil

GARNISH:

Diced avocados
Shredded cheddar cheese
Tortilla chips

Lime wedges
Cilantro leaves

Poach chicken breasts in stock until done, remove and shred or cut in pieces. Add tortilla pieces to stock and simmer 10 minutes until soft. Puree in blender and add back to pot with tomato puree and chicken pieces. Saute onions, garlic and peppers in oil. Add spices and Worcestershire sauce, and saute until fragrant. Add to soup and simmer 15 minutes. Garnish with cheese, avocado, tortilla chips, lime wedges and cilantro. Serves 8.

Recommended wine: Reserve Fumé

Mary Lannin
for
Murphy-Goode Estate Winery

Eggplant Soup

1 medium eggplant (approx 1 pound)
2 medium yellow onions, peeled and thinly sliced
1/3 cup shallots or scallions, minced
2 cups red bell pepper (approx 3 peppers), cored, seeded and chopped
6 cloves garlic, minced
1/3 cup light olive oil
1/2 teaspoon each dried whole basil, oregano and thyme

1/4 teaspoon red pepper flakes
3 cups diced tomatoes (canned or fresh)
2 quarts flavorful chicken or vegetable stock
1 cup Fumé Blanc
Creme frâiche or sour cream
Freshly chopped chives (garnish)

Slice unpeeled eggplant into rounds and place in one layer on a lightly oiled baking sheet. Saute onions, shallots or scallions, red bell pepper and garlic in the olive oil until soft, but not brown. Spread evenly over the top of the eggplant rounds and roast in preheated 425 degree oven for 15 to 20 minutes or until the eggplant is soft and lightly browned. Be careful that the topping doesn't burn.

In a food processor or blender, puree the eggplant with the herbs, pepper flakes, tomatoes, and stock. Place in a large soup pot with the wine, and gently reheat just to a boil. Correct seasoning and thin with additional stock if desired. Divide into bowls and garnish with a dollop of creme frâiche or sour cream and freshly chopped chives.

Serves 10 to 12.

Recommended Wine: Fetzer Valley Oaks Fumé Blanc.

Chef John Ash, Culinary Director
Fetzer Vineyards

John Ash, one of California's most influential chefs, helped to nurture a cuisine that has become international, in its usage of fresh, seasonal ingredients of the region of the chef. As Executive Chef of John Ash and Co., his own restaurant, he won countless awards for his innovative recipes. Now the Culinary Director for Fetzer Vineyards, he is heading the winery's food and wine educational program, nationally and internationally.

Tomato Provencal Soup

1 leek, diced
1 onion, chopped
4 cloves garlic, minced
1/2 fresh fennel bulb, chopped
2-3 tablespoons olive oil
8 tomatoes, skinned, seeded, chopped (or one 1 pound, 12 ounce can peeled tomatoes)
3 cups chicken stock
1/4 cup rice, uncooked
1 bay leaf
4-6 tablespoons fresh parsley, minced

1 tablespoon fresh basil, chopped (or 1 teaspoon dry)
2 teaspoons fresh thyme (or 1/2 teaspoon dry)
1 tablespoon fennel or anise seed
1 carrot, peeled and shredded or julienned
Pinch saffron
4 tablespoons tomato paste
1 teaspoon orange zest
Salt and fresh cracked pepper to taste

Peel tomatoes, cut in half and squeeze out the seeds and juice into a sieve set over a bowl. Dice tomato pulp. Chop onion, mince garlic and leeks, and peel and shred or julienne the carrot. Saute first 5 ingredients (leek, onion, garlic and fennel in olive oil) until tender, approximately 2 to 3 minutes.

Mix tomato pulp with the vegetables and stir over low heat for about one minute. Add juice from tomatoes and the chicken broth and bring to a boil. Then add rice and herbs. Simmer for 30 minutes. Stir in tomato paste, shredded carrot and orange zest, and remove from heat. Soup may be done ahead to this point and held (do not continue to cool or flavors lose their freshness).

Variations: Add 1/2 to 1 cup of shellfish (scallops, clams, shrimp, or crab) 5 to 7 minutes before serving; or top with tarragon flavored créme frâiche.

When ready to serve, garnish with freshly chopped parsley. Serves 6.

These flavors are typical of both Provence and California. The orange zest and licorice flavors (fennel, anise and/or tarragon) add a delicious accent. We sometimes vary the soup with the addition of shellfish or fish (mock Bouillabaisse) or a flavored créme frâiche.

Delicious with McDowell's Grenache Rosé.

Karen Keehn
McDowell Vineyards

Cream of Carrot Soup with Dill

2 pounds roughly chopped carrots
 (about 5-1/2 cups)
1/2 cup roughly chopped leek,
 white only
2 1/2 cups chicken stock, enough
 to barely cover the carrots and
 leeks
1/2 teaspoon salt
1 teaspoon Worcestershire sauce

2 tablespoons butter
2 tablespoons flour
3 cups milk
2 teaspoons chopped fresh
 dill weed
1/8 teaspoon white pepper
A few shakes of allspice or
 nutmeg
2 tablespoons dry sherry

Put the carrots, leeks, stock, salt and Worcestershire in a sauce pot. Bring to a boil, then reduce heat and simmer for twenty minutes, or until the carrots are quite tender. Allow to cool, then puree in a food processor, blender or food mill.

Make a roux of the butter and flour, stir in the milk and simmer for ten minutes. To this base, add the pureed carrot and seasonings. Bring slowly up to temperature. Add the sherry just before serving.

Chefs Robert Engel and Christine Topolos
Russian River Vineyards Restaurant

Pumpkin Soup with Apples and Black Walnuts

1 large onion, chopped
4 garlic cloves, minced
1 stick unsalted butter
1 1/2 pounds pumpkin, peeled, seeded and diced
4 Pippin apples, peeled, cored and sliced (or other tart cooking apple)
1 cup black walnuts, chopped
1 cup apple cider

5 cups chicken stock or canned broth
1 teaspoon crumbled sage
1/2 teaspoon fresh thyme leaves, chopped
Salt and white pepper to taste
1 cup heavy cream or half & half
1/2 cup black walnuts, finely chopped

Saute the onion and garlic in the butter over moderate heat, stirring until they are softened. Add the pumpkin, apples, walnuts, cider, stock, herbs and salt and pepper. Bring to a boil, reduce heat and simmer, partially covered, for about 45 minutes, or until pumpkin is tender.

Puree the mixture in batches. Transfer to a pot and stir in the cream, being careful not to let it boil. Garnish with finely chopped walnuts.

Serves 10.

Suggested wine: Rodney Strong Vineyards Chalk Hill Chardonnay.

Bea Beasley
for
Rodney Strong Vineyards

Jamaican Red Bean Soup

1 pound boneless smoked ham,
cut into 1/2-inch cubes
2 cans (15.5 ounces) red kidney
beans, drained and rinsed
2 cans (13 3/4 ounces) beef broth
2 cups potatoes, cut into 1/2-inch
cubes
2 cups sweet potatoes, cut in 1/2-
inch cubes
3/4 cup chopped celery

1 cup chopped onion
1 1/2 teaspoons thyme leaves,
crushed
1/2 teaspoon ground allspice
1/4 teaspoon ground red
pepper
1/4 teaspoon ground black
pepper
1 cup sweet Vermouth
2 tablespoons cornstarch

In a large saucepan, combine ham with 2 1/2 cups water, beans, broth, potatoes, sweet potatoes, celery, onion, thyme, allspice and red and black peppers. Bring to a boil. Reduce heat and simmer, covered, until potatoes are tender, about 25 minutes. Add Vermouth. In a cup, combine cornstarch with 1/2 cup cold water until smooth. Stir into soup and bring to a boil. Stir until slightly thickened, about 1 minutes.

Serves 6.

Beaucanon Winery

65

Red Bell Pepper Soup

2 tablespoons olive oil
2 pounds red bell peppers (approx 10-12 medium). Green bell peppers may be substituted, but they will not have the natural sweetness of the red.

1 onion, chopped
4 cloves garlic, chopped
4 cups chicken stock
2 teaspoons coriander, minced
6 tablespoons sour cream

Clean, de-seed and chop peppers. Saute onions, garlic and peppers in olive oil until tender (approximately 10 minutes) shaking pan occasionally to prevent burning. Add half the chicken stock and cook for ten more minutes.

At this point, either remove from heat to strain the mixture for a creamier texture, or leave as is for a chunkier-style soup.

Add the rest of the chicken stock and simmer until the desired consistency is reached. Season with coriander. For richer flavor, stir in cream. Remove from heat. Garnish each serving with 1 tablespoon sour cream. Serve hot or cold.   Serves 6.

Try with Fumé Blanc, Sauvignon Blanc.

California Culinary Academy Scholarship Winner
Beringer Vineyards

Sweet Pepper

Tomato Soup Fumé

1/2 cube butter
1/2 bell pepper, chopped
2 small onions, sliced
2 stalks celery, chopped
1/4 cup flour
1/2 cup Fumé Blanc
1 tablespoon fresh dill, or 1
 teaspoon dry
1/2 teaspoon basil
1/2 teaspoon thyme

1 teaspoon sugar
Salt and white pepper
4 pounds tomatoes peeled
 and chopped, 28 ounces, or
 1 large can tomatoes seeded
 and drained and 1 large can
 stewed tomatoes seeded and
 drained, liquids reserved
3 cups chicken stock

Saute onion and celery. Add flour, saute. Add wine and seasonings.
Add tomatoes and stock, and simmer 15 minutes. Add tomato juices.
Puree. Adjust seasonings, cool. Top bowls of soup with puff pastry*
and bake 15 to 20 minutes. Serves 8 to 10.

**Linda Hagen, Executive Chef
Chateau St. Jean**

*Ready-made puff pastry is available at specialty food stores or
supermarkets in the cooler cabinets. VMH*

Curried Carrot Soup

1 large onion, chopped	1 bay leaf
1 teaspoon minced garlic	1/8 teaspoon dried thyme,
1 teaspoon minced ginger root	crumbled
2 tablespoons unsalted butter	1/4 teaspoon ground pepper
1 teaspoon curry powder	1/2 cup half & half
1/8 teaspoon cinnamon	1 tablespoon honey
2 pounds carrots, peeled and	1/2 cup plain yogurt or heavy
chopped	cream
3 1/2 cups chicken stock	

In a kettle, cook onion, garlic and ginger in butter over moderate heat, stirring until onion is soft. Stir in curry powder and cinnamon and cook, stirring for 10 seconds. Add stock, bay leaf, carrots, thyme, pepper and 1/2 cup water. Bring to boil and simmer, covered, for 30 minutes.

Discard bay leaf. Let cool, then puree in blender, in 2 batches, until very smooth. Transfer to large saucepan and whisk in half & half, honey, and salt to taste, then heat. Top each serving with a dollop of yogurt or cream.   Makes 8 cups.

Landmark Vineyards

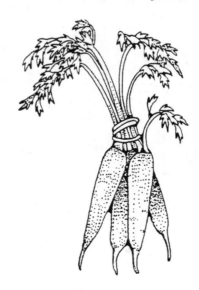

Salads

SPICES OF THE WORLD

Salad of Bitter and Exotic Greens
with Basil Oil and Blue Cheese

2 bunches basil
1 cup olive oil
1 head radicchio
1 head Belgian endive
2 bunches watercress or arugula
2 heads butter lettuce

1 tablespoon Champagne or
 white wine vinegar
Juice of 1/2 lemon
1 teaspoon salt
2-3 ounces blue cheese,
 crumbled

Remove leaves from one of the bunches of basil and reserve. Add stems to the second bunch of basil and blanch in 2 quarts boiling water for 15 seconds. Quickly refresh under cold running water, pat dry and coarsely chop. Measure the basil and place equal parts of basil and olive oil in a blender and make a smooth paste. Remove and add 3 parts oil to 1 part puree. Shake to combine thoroughly and let settle 24 hours. Strain clear oil through a paper coffee filter. Store tightly covered in the refrigerator for up to 1 week.

Rinse and thoroughly dry all salad greens. Keep small leaves whole; tear large leaves into pieces. Add reserved basil leaves.

Make a vinaigrette with 1/2 cup of the basil oil, Champagne vinegar, lemon juice and salt. Toss the lettuces and basil in vinaigrette and top with crumbled blue cheese. Serves 4.

Wine suggestion: Beringer Private Reserve Cabernet Sauvignon. The tannic backbone of the Private Reserve is softened by the cheese; the wine's lush varietal fruit makes a good foil for the greens and basil oil.

Jerry Comfort, Executive Chef
Beringer Vineyards

Warm Mushroom Salad with Champagne Vinaigrette and Goat Cheese Croutons

16 3/4-inch slices sourdough or
 French baguette
6 tablespoons butter, melted
8 tablespoons soft goat cheese (or
 any spreadable white cheese)
2 small heads red or green leaf
 lettuce, washed
1/2 pound fresh sliced mushrooms

1 cup extra virgin olive oil
1/2 cup Champagne
Zest of 2 lemons
1/2 teaspoon freshly ground
 black pepper
2 teaspoons salt

Preheat oven to 400 degrees.

Brush the bread with butter and toast in oven. Spread the croutons with the cheese. Set aside.

Tear the lettuce into bite-size pieces and place in a mixing bowl.

In a small saucepan over medium heat, whisk together the olive oil, champagne, lemon zest, black pepper and salt. Heat until simmering, then add the mushrooms.

Pour the warm mushroom dressing over the lettuce and toss. Serve immediately, garnishing with the croutons.   Serves 8.

Serve with Korbel Champagne/Natural.

Teresa Douglas/Mitchell, Culinary Director
Korbel Champagne Cellars

A graduate of the California Culinary Academy, Ms. Douglas/Mitchell served an apprenticeship with Bradley Ogden, then became Chef at the Vintner's Inn, then with John Ash & Company, prior to her present position at Korbel Champagne Cellars, where she is responsible for the pairing of menus with Korbel Champagnes.

Oven-Dried Tomatoes with Herb Dressing

6 large ripe Roma tomatoes, cut in half
1/4 cup olive oil

Rub each tomato half with olive oil and place on a sheet pan. Season each with salt and pepper. Place in a 200 degree oven for 5 to 6 hours, until they are half dried. Chill.

HERB DRESSING:

1/2 cup Chardonnay	1 teaspoon fresh thyme
1/2 cup olive oil	2 tablespoons fresh parsley
1 tablespoon fresh basil	2 cloves garlic, peeled
1 tablespoon fresh oregano	

Puree all the ingredients in a blender.

To serve, place tomatoes on salad greens, ladle a small amount of the dressing on each oven-dried tomato. Garnish with a grind of fresh black pepper.   Serves 6.

Elaine Bell, Culinary Director
Sterling Vineyards

A native of Sonoma, Elaine Bell studied Nutrition and Food Science at Humboldt State University. She is a graduate of the Culinary Institute of America at Hyde Park, New York. Her professional experience of 11 years includes three years at Domaine Chandon Restaurant in Yountville and the Spa at the Sonoma Mission Inn, where she helped design the menus and recipes.

Elaine's cooking style is similar to the wines she represents -- balance, elegance and tastiness are the hallmarks of her cooking.

Baked Chevre Salad with Fuji Apples and Candied Pecans

8 cups mixed greens
2 fuji apples
1 cup pecans
1/4 cup plus 3 tablespoons butter
1/2 cup sugar
10 ounces chevre cheese
2 cups fresh bread crumbs
1/2 cup safflower oil

2 tablespoons blackberry
 vinegar
3 tablespoons sparkling wine
3 tablespoons fresh thyme
 (chopped very fine)
Salt and freshly ground
 pepper to taste

TO CANDY THE PECANS:

Melt the 3 tablespoons butter in a medium saute pan on low heat. Add the pecans and stir constantly with wooden spoon for the next 10 minutes. Pecans should get to be golden color and may appear a little darker, but do not let them burn. At this point, start to add the sugar gradually and continue to stir. You will have a caramel type mixture when the butter marries with the sugar and pecans, but be sure you do not overcook the mixture. Take pecans off heat and pour onto a small sheet pan lined with parchment paper. Try to keep the pecans separate from each other so you can present them well. Lightly salt. After mixture has cooled for about 10 minutes, you can start to break apart the pieces that stuck together.

TO BREAD THE CHEVRE:

Portion the chevre into 4 equal pieces. Mold each piece into a thick patty shape. Dip each patty into the safflower oil, then dip into the bread crumbs. You will want to cover the entire piece of cheese with bread crumbs, so be sure and pack the bread crumbs firmly with the palm of your hand. Transfer the breaded chevre onto a sheet pan lined with parchment or foil. Preheat oven to 350 degrees.

TO PREPARE SALAD:

Start by placing the chevre in preheated oven. Chevre should be baked for 10 minutes, so while it is in the oven, you can be preparing the rest of the salad.

Cut the fuji apples into 1/4-inch slices and set aside. Melt the 1/4 cup butter in a medium saute pan on low heat. Once the butter is completely melted, add the apples and cook for about 4 minutes. The apple slices should appear to have little extra color, but you do not want them to be too soft. Once you have cooked the apples for the 4 minutes, put them in a stainless steel bowl. Add the mixed greens, blackberry vinegar, sparkling wine and fresh thyme. Toss salad with tongs until it is well incorporated. Taste for salt and pepper and season.

Remove baked chevre from oven when it has been in the oven for the full 10 minutes. Portion the greens mixture onto 4 plates and place the baked chevre on top of the salad. Place about 6 candied pecans around each salad. You can add more if you would like. Serves 4.

Sit back and enjoy this wonderful salad with a glass of Domaine Carneros Sparkling Wine!

This is a great combination of flavors and is a really simple salad to prepare for either a first course or as an entree salad. The chevre, combined with the fuji apples and fresh thyme, complements the delicate qualities in sparkling wine. And the candied pecans will always please your guests and keep them coming back for more!

Trish Thomas, Chef
Domaine Carneros

Artichokes Stuffed with Smoldering Shrimp

Boil 12 artichokes until done, and drain upside down in refrigerator overnight.

2 red bell peppers, peeled by roasting
1 1/2 pounds cream cheese
1/4 cup mayonnaise
1 cup finely minced white onion
3 tablespoons butter
1/2 teaspoon cayenne pepper, or to taste

1 tablespoon thyme leaves to taste
1/2 teaspoon oregano leaves
6 cloves garlic
2 pounds bay shrimp
1/3 cup celery

In sauce pan, melt butter, then saute onions and celery until slightly translucent. Add garlic, then thyme, oregano and cayenne. Saute slightly, then remove from heat.

Blend cream cheese, mayonnaise and bell peppers in food processor. When finished, remove from food processor to bowl. Then add all other ingredients. Mix well and refrigerate.

Stuff artichokes and serve. Top with a slight amount of finely chopped parsley.   Serves 12.

Serve with Heitz Cellar Napa Valley Chardonnay.

Kathleen Heitz Myers
Heitz Wine Cellars

Orange Pecan Chicken
on Tender Salad Greens

8 cups broken leaves of tender mild butter lettuce (loosely pack to measure)

10 ounces moist cooked skinless chicken breast meat, cooled, torn into lengthwise strips 1 1/2 by 1/8 inches

2 teaspoons minced fresh marjoram leaves (or crumbled dry marjoram)

2 teaspoons grated fresh orange peel

1/4 teaspoon crushed dry hot red pepper (to taste)

Lemon Dressing

Salt

1/2 cup very fresh crisp pecans, cut into lengthwise slivers

Gently turn all ingredients except nuts and salt with enough dressing to cloak generously, and salt to season well. Arrange on four dinner plates. Sprinkle with nuts. Makes 3 to 4 main course servings. Accompany with crisply crusted French rolls.

LEMON DRESSING:

2 tablespoons fresh lemon juice
1 teaspoon sugar
1/2 teaspoon salt

1 teaspoon minced green onions (white part only)
1/2 cup light olive oil

Combine first 4 ingredients. Gradually whisk in olive oil.

Serve with Monterey Vineyards Classic White.

Shirley Sarvis, Consultant and Food Writer
for
Monterey Vineyards

Raspberry Rose Salad

6 large handfuls of red leaf
lettuces -- oak leaf, lolla rosa,
radicchio, etc.
1 cup fresh raspberries
3 edible pink or rose-colored roses
(raised without herbicides or
pesticides)

1 1/2 tablespoons raspberry
vinegar *
5 tablespoons vegetable oil
Salt and pepper to taste

Wash and dry the lettuces, and tear into bite-size pieces, if necessary.

Remove petals from roses.

Toss greens with the oil until well coated, then sprinkle on vinegar, salt,
pepper, and raspberries and toss again.

Divide among six salad plates and scatter rose petals over each.
Serves 6.

* A raspberry vinegar made with a white wine base is preferable for this
dish. Kozlowski Farms in Forestville, California, makes an excellent one,
and will ship it to you if you cannot find it in your marketplace.

Serve with Simi Rosé of Cabernet Sauvignon Wine.

Mary Evely, Chef
Simi Winery

Mediterranean Pasta Salad

PASTA:

1 pound fusilli or corkscrew pasta
3 tablespoons extra virgin olive oil
3 tablespoons Brut Champagne
Salt to taste

OTHER INGREDIENTS:

6 cups plum tomatoes, quartered
1/2 cup black olives (Kalamata, for
example) sliced
1/2 cup green olives (Sicilian are
good) sliced
1/2 cup basil, chopped
1 cup scallions, finely sliced
1/4 cup capers

1/4 pancetta, cooked and
crumbled (optional)
1/2 cup extra virgin olive oil
2 tablespoons Balsamic
vinegar
1 teaspoon ground tumeric
2 teaspoons ground cumin
Salt and freshly ground black
pepper to taste

Cook the pasta in lots of boiling water until tender, but with a little bite.
Place in an ice water bath to stop the cooking process. Drain and toss
with half the olive oil and the seasonings.

Combine the other ingredients and toss to coat them with the rest of
the oil. Add this mixture to the pasta.

Refrigerate if serving in more than an hour. Otherwise, serve this salad
room temperature as an accompaniment to grilled fish or chicken.

Serves 10.

Serve with Korbel Champagne/Brut.

Teresa Douglas/Mitchell, Culinary Director
Korbel Champagne Cellars

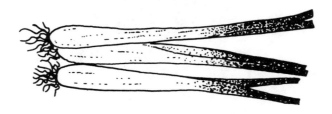

Baby Lettuce Salad
with Prawns and Grapefruit

4 cups mixed baby lettuces, washed thoroughly and dried

16 medium prawns, peeled and de-veined

16 pink grapefruit sections

1 cup Sauvignon Blanc

1 teaspoon chopped fresh (or 1/2 teaspoon dried) tarragon

1 teaspoon minced fresh chives

1 cup light olive oil

Poach prawns in the wine with 1/2 of the herbs, until prawns turn just barely pink. Remove from heat and let cool in the liquid while washing the lettuce and preparing the grapefruit sections.

Drain prawns, reserving the liquid. Strain into a small saucepan and reduce over medium heat until liquid is about 1/4 cup. Let cool, then whisk in olive oil until thickened. Add tarragon, salt and pepper as needed.

Place lettuce on 4 chilled salad plates. Arrange prawns and grapefruit in alternating circle on each plate. Drizzle with dressing and sprinkle with the chopped chives. Serves 4.

Serve with Raymond Sauvignon Blanc.

Kas McGregor, Hospitality Director
Raymond Vineyard and Cellar

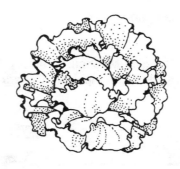

Spaghetti Fresci with Shrimp

1 pound spaghetti noodles
1 pound cooked bay shrimp
1/2 cup mayonnaise (or to taste)
1/4 cup white wine
Juice of 1-2 lemons
1 green bell pepper, finely
  chopped

1 red bell pepper, finely
  chopped
1 cup celery, finely chopped
3 green onions, minced
Zest of 1 lemon
1 tablespoon tarragon, minced
1 tablespoon parsley, minced

Cook the spaghetti until tender. Drain and rinse. Combine the shrimp, mayonnaise, wine, lemon juice, chopped vegetables, lemon zest and herbs. Blend thoroughly with the cooked spaghetti. Chill several hours before serving.   Serves 4.

Serve with Louis M. Martini Sauvignon Blanc.

Louis M. Martini Winery

Easy Three Bean Salad

SALAD:

1 1-pound can each, kidney
  beans, pinto beans, garbanzo
  beans, and corn
1/2 cup sliced green onion
1 cup celery, diced
1/4 cup chopped parsley
4 ounces diced green chilies

DRESSING:

3/4 cup oil
1/2 cup vinegar
1 large garlic clove, chopped
1 1/2 teaspoons salt
1 teaspoon chili powder
1 teaspoon oregano
1/4 teaspoon ground cumin
1/8 teaspoon tabasco

Discard the liquid from all the cans, rinse contents and drain. Mix with remaining ingredients in large bowl. Add dressing and chill 6 hours or overnight.

Serve with Louis Kunde Founder's Reserve Gewurztraminer 1992.

Jane Kunde
Kunde Estate Winery

Spicy Black Bean Salad

5 cups cooked black beans
1 red onion, minced
2 large tomatoes, seeded and
chopped
1/2 cup chopped fresh cilantro or
flat-leaf parsley
3 jalapeno peppers, seeded and
minced
3 cloves garlic, minced

2 tablespoons lemon or lime
juice
1 1/2 teaspoons ground cumin
2 tablespoons red wine
vinegar
1/2 cup olive oil
1 teaspoon salt
1/4 teaspoon ground pepper

Rinse the black beans under cold, running water. Drain thoroughly. In a large mixing bowl, combine beans with all other ingredients, tossing gently until mixed. This salad can be covered and refrigerated for up to 2 days. Season with salt and pepper to taste before serving.

Serves 10 to 12.

Serve with Cabernet Franc.

**Madelene Lyon, Tasting Room Manager
Konocti Winery**

Pastas
and
Grains

SPICES OF THE WORLD

Cheese Tortellini with a Pesto Cream Sauce and Grilled Chicken

9-10 ounces fresh cheese tortellini
1 whole boneless, skinless chicken breast, grilled and sliced julienne
1/8 yellow bell pepper, roasted, skin removed and sliced julienne
1/8 red bell pepper, roasted, skin removed and sliced julienne
1 cup tightly packed fresh basil leaves
1 clove minced garlic

1 tablespoon extra virgin olive oil
4 walnut halves
1 tablespoon freshly grated Parmesan cheese
1/2 pound unsalted butter
1 pint heavy whipping cream
2 tablespoons olive oil for the pasta water
1 tablespoon salt for the pasta water

Make the pesto first by adding the following ingredients into a food processor: basil leaves, garlic, 1 tablespoon extra virgin olive oil, walnuts and Parmesan cheese. Process for 1 minute.

On the stove top in a medium saucepan, melt the unsalted butter. When melted, add the heavy whipping cream, whisking while it comes to a boil. Simmer for 5 minutes and add pesto sauce. Bring to a second boil and reduce heat to a simmer for 20 to 30 minutes.

In a large saucepan, bring 3 quarts of water to a boil with 2 tablespoons extra virgin olive oil and the salt. Add tortellini and cook for 5 to 8 minutes or until tender, but firm. Drain the water and place the tortellini back in the same warm saucepan. Add the pesto cream sauce and the julienne chicken breast and toss gently. Divide into six portions and garnish with criss-crossed julienne red and yellow bell peppers.   Serves 6.

Serve with Chateau St. Jean Fumé Blanc.

Sandra Pessner, Chef de Cuisine
for
Chateau St. Jean

Zinfandel Noodles

6 egg yolks
2 whole eggs
1/4 cup Zinfandel
2 teaspoons olive oil
3/4 teaspoon salt

About 3 1/2 cups flour
Chopped fresh rosemary to
  taste (it's powerful, you may
  need only a teaspoon or so)
Melted butter

With a wire whisk, beat together first five ingredients until well blended. Pour into flour. Mix with a heavy spoon until it begins to hold together. Turn out onto a floured board and knead until very smooth and elastic, about 10 minutes.

Cut into sixths and roll thin. Cut by hand or hand-operated noodle machine (following machine instructions). Let the cut noodles dry over a wooden stick for about 1 hour. You may then freeze individual portions on a cookie sheet and later store in a plastic bag in the freezer for future use. Makes about 8 cups cooked noodles.

Serves 6 to 8.

To cook: Bring at least 4 quarts of water to a boil. Add 1 tablespoon salt and olive oil. Drop noodles into rapidly boiling water and cook for 2 to 3 minutes. Drain well and serve with melted butter and chopped fresh rosemary to taste.

Laura Spinetta
Charles Spinetta Winery and Gallery

Wild Mushroom Ravioli with White Truffle Oil

Sheets of herbed pasta -- use your favorite pasta recipe and add freshly chopped herbs, or buy.

MUSHROOM FILLING:

1 pound wild mushrooms, chantrelles, oyster cinnamon caps, porcinis, etc., cleaned and chopped
3 shallots, finely minced
2 ounces havarti cheese, grated
2 ounces romano cheese, finely grated
3-4 ounces marscapone
4 ounces marsala wine
Salt and pepper

Saute shallots in olive oil till clear and add mushrooms and cook till just done. Take off heat, cool and then add cheeses. Reduce marsala to a glaze and add to mushrooms. Correct seasoning. Lay out pasta sheets, place 1 heaping tablespoon of filling inside a 3-inch square, brush edges of pasta with egg wash, and cover with top sheet of pasta. Press air out gently and cut. Other shapes and designs work well, too. Dust lightly with flour and let sit 1 hour. Bring 3 to 4 quarts water to boil. Put in some of the raviolis (don't get too crowded) and turn down to barely a simmer. Cool 3 to 4 minutes to al dente. Remove and mix with sauce, and then drizzle white truffle oil generously on top.

SAUCE:

1 cup Madeira wine
1 1/2 cups veal demi glace (or mixture of chicken and beef)
White truffle oil

Bring 1/2 cup Madeira and 3/4 cup veal demi glace to boil and reduce to glaze and caramelize a bit in pan. Watch carefully. Add remaining Madeira and veal demi glace and thicken if necessary with arrowroot mixed with water. Check seasonings.

Serve with Matanzas Creek Sonoma County Sauvignon Blanc.

Sarah Kaswan, Chef
Matanzas Creek Winery

Spaghetti Primavera

1 pound hot Italian sausage
2 cloves garlic, minced
1 28-ounce can Italian plum
tomatoes, drained and chopped
1 cup finely chopped parsley
1 sprig fresh oregano (or 1
teaspoon dried)
Salt
Freshly ground black pepper

1 pound dried Italian
spaghettini
1/2 pound tender, young
zucchini, thinly sliced
3 red bell peppers, thinly
sliced
1/4 cup fresh basil, chopped
3/4 cup freshly grated
Parmesan cheese

Cover sausages in water. Boil until cooked, about 30 minutes. Remove, peel and slice thinly. Heat 2 tablespoons of oil in heavy skillet over medium heat. Add sausage and brown over medium-high heat. Remove. Discard all but 2 tablespoons of fat from skillet.

Add garlic and saute until transparent -- do not brown. Add tomatoes, parsley, oregano, salt and pepper. Cover and simmer gently for 15 minutes. Watch carefully, and stir from time to time. Add a little water if it gets too dry. Add sausage, cover and keep warm.

Cook the spaghettini according to directions while you complete the sauce.

Meanwhile, in another skillet, add the remaining 2 tablespoons oil and heat to medium high. Dry the snow peas on paper towels. Add the zucchini and red bell peppers to the skillet and saute a few minutes. Then add the snow peas and cook until they turn bright green. Add the vegetables to the sauce and toss thoroughly with the pasta and basil.

Sprinkle with parsley and Parmesan. Pass additional Parmesan cheese and serve with French bread.

Serve with Louis M. Martini Cabernet Sauvignon.

Louis M. Martini Winery

Pappardelle with Sweet Red Peppers

6-8 sweet red peppers
4 tablespoons olive oil
2 medium onions, chopped
1 tablespoon fresh basil, chopped
2 garlic cloves, finely chopped
1 cup beef or chicken stock

1 1/2 pounds fresh pasta cut
  in wide strips, or 1 pound
  dried wide noodles
1/2 cup sundried tomatoes
  packed in oil, chopped
1/2 cup toasted pine nuts

Char peppers on all sides, either over an open flame or under the broiler. Place still-hot peppers in a brown paper bag to steam for 5 minutes. When cool enough to handle, remove the charred skin, seeds and top, and chop coarsely. Reserve.

Saute onion in 2 tablespoons of the olive oil until translucent. Add the chopped peppers, garlic and herbs and remaining oil; saute a few minutes, then add stock. Cook over medium heat for 10 to 15 minutes until tender. Reserve 1/3 of the mixture, puree the rest in a food processor.

Cook pasta in a large pot of boiling water until tender. Toss with the pureed pepper mixture. Fold in reserved pepper pieces and sundried tomatoes. Season to taste with salt and pepper. Garnish with toasted pine nuts and serve. Serves 8.

Serve with Louis M. Martini Gamay Beaujolais.

Louis M. Martini Winery

Lovely fresh flavors combine for rave reviews on this dish.

*Sweet
Pepper*

Wild Mushroom Ravioli

PASTA:

1 cup all purpose flour	1 cup semolina
2 eggs	1 tablespoon olive oil
1/4 cup water	

In mixer with paddles, combine flours, add egg and olive oil until resembles a course crumb. Add water by tablespoons until mixed. Change to dough hook and knead for 5 minutes. Wrap in plastic and refrigerate.

Note: Pasta should be removed from refrigerator approximately one hour before needed.

MUSHROOM FILLING:

2 tablespoons oil	1 bay leaf
1/4 cup chopped onion or shallot	2 pounds wild mushrooms
2 tablespoons chopped garlic	1 tablespoon fresh thyme,
1 tablespoon fresh rosemary,	chopped
chopped	1/4 teaspoon cayenne pepper
1/2 teaspoon coriander, ground	1 cup cream

Saute onion and garlic in large pan until transparent. Add mushrooms and all spices. Cook for 5 to 7 minutes, stirring occasionally. Add cream and cook until cream binds all. Remove from heat and cover.

LEEK CREAM SAUCE:

1 tablespoon oil	3 leeks
3 cups cream	1/4 teaspoon white pepper
1/4 teaspoon salt	

In saucepan, saute leeks in oil, approximately 2 minutes. Add salt and pepper. Add cream and slow boil for 10 minutes. Place in blender and puree all approximately 1 minute. Strain mixture through fine strainer, and return liquid to pan. Set aside on very low heat.

Roll pasta in machine to thinnest setting. Cut pasta into 3-inch squares or circles, 2 per ravioli. Cook pasta in salted boiling water until al dente. Drain and oil. Ladle leek cream onto bottom of plate and place one piece of pasta on cream. Spoon mushroom filling onto pasta and top with pasta square/round. Garnish with finely diced red peppers.   Serves 4 to 6.

Serve with Monticello Cellars Domaine Montreaux.

David Lawson, Chef
Monticello Cellars

Fresh Basil and Tomatoes Pasta

1 1/2 pounds ripe Roma tomatoes,
 coarsely chopped *
1 bunch basil leaves, sliced
julienne
2 cloves fresh garlic, crushed
1 teaspoon salt
1/2 teaspoon crushed peppercorns

1/4 teaspoon dried oregano
Pinch of crushed dried red
 chile peppers
1 pound pasta
Freshly grated Parmesan
 cheese

Combine the tomatoes and spices in large bowl, cover. Let stand at room temperature for 1 hour. Cook pasta, al dente. Drain. To serve, top hot pasta with sauce and sprinkle with Parmesan cheese.

                                                        Serves 4 to 6

* Fresh garden tomatoes may be substituted.

Serve with Cline Cellars '91 Cotes D'Oakley.

Nicki Spedus
for
Cline Cellars

Polenta with Italian Sausage

4 sweet red peppers, coarsely chopped
2 medium onions, coarsely chopped
4 cloves garlic, minced
4 medium zucchini, cubed
1/2 cup fresh (or 3 tablespoons dried) basil leaves, roughly chopped

1 cup red or white wine
8 mild or hot Italian sausages
2 cups coarse stone-ground yellow cornmeal or polenta flour
1 tablespoon butter

Place the cubed and chopped vegetables into a large roasting pan. Add the basil leaves, and salt and pepper. Place the sausages on top of the vegetables and puncture them several times with a fork. Roast in a 425 degree oven for 30 to 40 minutes, or until done. Deglaze the pan with the wine and hold in a warm oven.

Bring 4 cups of water to a boil, add the polenta a little at a time, whisking continually. When you have added all the polenta, add butter, then lower the heat and continue stirring until the mixture has thickened, about 10 minutes. Pour polenta into a bowl or onto a wooden platter.

Serve topped with the sausage and vegetable mixture.   Serves 6.

For even creamier polenta, fold in a few 1/4-inch slices of Teleme Jack cheese as it begins to thicken.

Serve with Louis M. Martini Merlot.

Louis M. Martini Winery

Onion

Pasta With Scallops in
Lemon Herb Cream Sauce

1/2 cup butter
1/2 cup Fumé Blanc
1 clove garlic, minced
2 shallots, finely minced
2 cups cream

1 tablespoon lemon zest
1/2 pound scallops
2 teaspoons marjoram,
 chopped
Pasta, 2-4 ounces per person

Wash, dry and chop fresh herb. (Choose one: Marjoram, fennel, tarragon or basil to complement Fumé Blanc.)

Melt butter in non-corrosive saucepan and saute garlic and shallots for two minutes or until golden. Add scallops and saute, coating with butter.

Add Fumé Blanc and poach for 3 to 5 minutes. Take care not to overcook or the scallops will toughen. Remove scallops and keep warm. Reduce liquid by one-third.

Add cream, reduce for twenty minutes; however, during the last five minutes, add fresh herbs and lemon zest, and stir until warmed through. Fold in scallops and toss with pasta.

While the sauce is reducing, cook pasta until "just" done. Drain and rinse quickly with warm water. Shake out excess water. Coat with one or two tablespoons of olive oil. (For added interest, use herb or red bell pepper pasta.)

Toss pasta with sauce and garnish with fresh herbs, lemon zest or chopped red and yellow pepper, and fresh cracked pepper. Serves 2.

Serve with McDowell Fumé Blanc.

Richard Keehn, Proprietor
McDowell Valley Vineyards

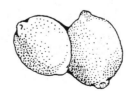

Saffron Risotto

4 tablespoons unsalted butter
1/2 onion, chopped
1 2/3 cups Arborio rice
1/2 cup Chardonnay

Generous pinch powdered
saffron
4 cups low-salt chicken broth,
heated to the simmering
point

Melt butter in a heavy pan. Add onions and saute until golden. Add rice and stir to coat all the grains with butter. Pour in the wine and cook, stirring until evaporated.

Dissolve saffron in a little of the hot broth and add to rice. Add remaining broth a little at a time, stirring often. You will need to regulate the heat to the point where the rice is just barely bubbling throughout this procedure.

As soon as all the stock is incorporated into the rice, adjust the seasoning and serve immediately. Or, proceed with recipe for saffron rice cakes.   Serves 4.

**Mary Evely, Chef
Simi Winery**

Fettucini with Sundried Tomatoes, California Prunes and Mustard

1/3 cup leeks (1 leek) chopped
1 tablespoon minced garlic
1/2 cup fresh parsley, chopped
1/2 cup fresh basil, chopped
1 cup fresh zucchini, chopped
3/4 cup wild mushrooms, chopped
3 tablespoons sundried tomatoes, chopped
2 tablespoons Mendocino Mustard

4 large California pitted prunes, chopped
1/2 cup pecans, chopped
2 tablespoons butter, plus 1 tablespoon olive oil
2 tablespoons Zinfandel or Rhone varietal wine
4-5 ounces fettucini pasta

In a large pot, bring salted water to a boil in preparation for cooking pasta. Dice all vegetables, herbs and nuts; keep separate. Mix together the chopped sundried tomatoes, chopped prunes and Mendocino mustard. Set aside.

In saute pan over medium heat, melt butter and oil together, and saute the leeks and zucchini for 3 to 4 minutes. Add minced garlic and saute for 30 seconds, then add basil and mushrooms and saute for 1 minute before adding the tomato/prune mixture. Saute all for 1 to 2 minutes more. The pan will start to brown on the bottom. Remove vegetables and keep warm.

Begin cooking pasta. While pasta is cooking, add 1 tablespoon butter to saute pan to loosen pan drippings; then splash pan with red wine and deglaze. Return vegetables to pan to reheat and coat for several seconds; turn off heat. Quickly drain pasta and rinse under hot water; shake to remove all water, then toss with light coat of olive oil. Put pasta on hot plates and add fresh cracked black pepper and spoon vegetables on top. Sprinkle with fresh parsley and chopped pecans. Serve immediately.   Serves 2.

Serve with McDowell Zinfandel or Les Vieux Cepages Le Tresor, Syrah, Bistro Red or Bistro Syrah.

Richard Keehn, Proprietor
McDowell Valley Vineyards

Fettucini in Basil Cream

3 tablespoons olive oil
3 tablespoons butter
1-2 cloves garlic, minced
3-4 tomatoes, peeled, seeded and
 chopped
1/2 cup dry white wine
1/2 cup heavy cream

1/2 cup finely chopped fresh
 basil leaves
Salt and white pepper to taste
1 pound fettucine (fresh is
 best)
Freshly grated Parmesan
 cheese

Heat oil and butter in a heavy saucepan over medium heat. Gently saute garlic for a minute, then add tomatoes. Simmer until they soften, then add wine and cream. Simmer 5 to 10 minutes or until sauce becomes consistency of heavy cream. Add chopped basil and simmer another 2 to 3 minutes. Add salt and white pepper to taste.

In large kettle, cook the fettucine in boiling, salted water with a tablespoon of oil. When it has reached the "al dente" stage (still firm to the bite), drain immediately.

Add the sauce to the hot fettucine, toss and serve immediately on warm plates. Add a leaf or two of basil to each serving for garnish. Pass a bowl of freshly grated Parmesan cheese.

Serve with Eberle Chardonnay.

Gary Eberle
Eberle Winery

Basil

Linguini with Clams Monterey

1/4 cup olive oil
1 large onion, diced
3 cloves garlic, minced
1/2 cup chopped parsley
2 tablespoons chopped fresh basil
(or 1 teaspoon dried)
6 sliced mushrooms (approx 1 cup)
1/4 cup dry white wine

2 cans (6.5 ounces each) minced or chopped clams
1/2 tablespoon chopped fresh oregano
1/4 cup freshly grated Parmesan cheese
Dash cayenne
1 pound linguini

Saute onions and garlic in olive oil over medium-high heat in heavy saute pan until golden. Add chopped parsley, mushrooms and basil. Saute for approximately 3 minutes until blended. Splash white wine into mixture and simmer until reduced by 1/2. Add clams with their juices, the oregano and cayenne. Season to taste with salt and pepper.

After mixture has returned to a simmer, stir in Parmesan and continue to simmer, uncovered. Prepare pasta according to package directions in boiling water, with 1 tablespoon olive oil until al dente.

Drain pasta and add clam mixture. Sprinkle liberally with grated Parmesan or Asiago and serve. Serves 4.

This is especially good served with a green salad, crusty sourdough bread and a chilled Sauvignon Blanc.

Duane Bue

An innovative chef who is at home with virtually any cuisine, Duane Bue is a Realtor here in the California Wine Country.

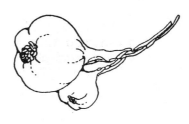

Saffron Rice Cakes with
Fontina and Asiago Cheeses

4 cups cooked Saffron Risotto
3 ounces Italian Fontina cheese
2 tablespoons unsalted butter

1 ounce freshly grated Asiago
cheese

Spread risotto out on a baking sheet to cool. Cut cheese into 8 rounded slices. Form rice into 8 cakes enclosing a slice of cheese in each.

Heat butter in a saute pan until foaming, then add the cakes. To prevent the cakes from sticking, shake the pan every minute until a crust begins to form (about 3 to 4 minutes). Continue cooking over medium heat until the cakes are a deep golden brown, about 10 minutes. Turn and cook the other side in the same manner.

Drain cakes briefly on a paper towel, then place 2 cakes on each warmed plate, scatter some grated Asiago over and serve immediately.
Serves 4.

Serving suggestion: These rice cakes are so rich that I recommend serving them with a fresh tomato salsa, or just slices of vine-ripened tomato with some chopped fresh basil, salt and pepper.

This recipe combines ideas from two traditional Italian rice dishes. It is so good, I always make sure to have leftovers when I make risotto.

Serve with Simi Chardonnay.

Mary Evely, Chef
Simi Winery

Saffron

Bow Tie Pasta with
Chicken, Mushrooms and Artichokes

1 medium onion, finely chopped
3 cloves garlic, finely minced
1 tablespoon oregano, minced
1 tablespoon basil, minced
2 tablespoons olive oil
2 cups sliced mushrooms
3 8-ounce cans tomato sauce
1 14-ounce can quartered
 artichoke hearts (non-marinated)

6 slices of prosciutto, finely
 sliced
1/2 cup half & half cream
4 skinless, boneless grilled
 chicken breasts
1 package bow tie pasta (12
 ounces)
Parmesan cheese

Saute onion and garlic in olive oil until soft; add herbs and mushrooms and saute until mushrooms are lightly browned. Add tomato sauce, prosciutto and artichokes and simmer about 20 minutes. Just before serving, add half & half. Top sauced pasta with grilled chicken breasts and Parmesan cheese.   Serves 6.

Serve with Murphy-Goode Chardonnay.

Mary Lannin
for
Murphy-Goode Estate Winery

Herb Pasta with Braised Duck Sauce and Cracklings

PASTA:

1 cup fresh oregano and thyme
leaves
1 egg

1 tablespoon olive oil
1 teaspoon salt
1 1/2 cups all-purpose flour

SAUCE:

6 duck legs
3 cups chicken or duck stock
1 ounce dried porcini mushrooms
1/4 cup olive oil
1 large red or yellow onion, thinly
sliced
2 sweet red peppers, seeded and
julienned
3 large tomatoes, seeded and
diced

3 cloves garlic, minced
2 small yellow squash, thinly
sliced
2 small zucchini, thinly sliced
3 carrots, cut into thin strips
3 tablespoons minced fresh
oregano and thyme, with
extra sprigs for garnish
Salt and freshly ground
pepper to taste

Place the cup of herbs in the bowl of a food processor and mince fine. Add the egg, olive oil and salt, and process. Add 1 cup of the flour and process. Add the remaining flour in small increments, processing after each addition until the dough forms a ball. Test the dough by pinching after each flour addition. It should feel smooth and elastic and not stick to your fingers. When you reach this point, let dough rest, covered, for 15 minutes. Then roll and cut for fettucini.

Remove skin from duck legs and cut into large dice. Place in a heavy skillet with a cup of water, bring to a boil, then reduce to a simmer. Cook slowly until cracklings are golden brown. (This will take at least an hour.) Remove with a slotted spoon to paper towels to drain, salt lightly, and set aside.

In the meantime, place the duck legs and stock in a saucepan, bring to a boil, then reduce to a simmer and cook for about an hour, until meat is very tender.

Remove duck legs from stock. Add the dried mushrooms to the hot stock and let them soften for 15 minutes. Remove, squeezing out excess liquid, and mince. Remove duck meat from bones.

In a large saute pan, heat the olive oil and add the onion, peppers and mushrooms. Saute for 3 minutes, stirring occasionally. Add the stock, garlic and tomatoes, and boil for 5 minutes. Add the duck meat, yellow and green squash, carrots and herbs, and simmer for 2 to 3 more minutes. Season with salt and pepper to taste.

Cook pasta in a large pot of boiling, salted water until al dente. (This will take less than a minute with fresh pasta.) Serve with the sauce and garnish with cracklings and herb sprigs. Serves 6.

Serve with Simi Cabernet Sauvignon Wine.

Mary Evely, Chef
Simi Winery

Spaghetti al Fromaggio

1 pound ground beef
1/2 cup chopped onion
1/4 cup chopped green pepper
1 small clove garlic, crushed
1 can (1 pound) tomatoes
1 can (6 ounces) tomato paste
1 teaspoon salt
1/2 teaspoon basil, crushed
1/2 teaspoon oregano, crushed

1 cup (4 ounces) shredded
Sonoma Jack Cheese
1/4 cup grated Sonoma Dry
Jack Cheese
1 package (7-8 ounces) thin
spaghetti
Grated Sonoma Dry Jack
cheese

Cook beef with onion, green pepper and garlic in large skillet until meat is browned. Stir in tomatoes, tomato paste, salt, oregano and basil. Simmer 30 minutes. Just before serving, stir in Sonoma Jack cheese and Sonoma Dry Jack cheese. Makes 4 cups sauce.

Meanwhile, prepare spaghetti according to package directions; drain. Turn spaghetti onto heated platter. Serve sauce over spaghetti with additional Sonoma Dry Jack cheese. Serves 4 to 6.

Sonoma Cheese Factory

It's the third generation of the Viviani family now making Sonoma Jack and Sonoma Cheddar cheeses at their place on the Plaza in Sonoma. Winners of many prizes in national and international judgings, their cheeses are now shipped world-wide.

Green Pasta with Herbs

1 pound fusilli noodles
2 tablespoons butter
2 tablespoons olive oil
4 cloves garlic, crushed
1 cup dry white wine
3 twists of a pepper grinder

1 tablespoon red chili powder
1 cup mixed basil, mint and
 parsley, finely chopped
Salt and pepper to taste
Romano cheese

Cook the noodles until tender. Keep warm.

Melt the butter and olive oil in a large skillet. Add the garlic and cook over low heat until it begins to brown slightly. Add the wine and cook until liquid is reduced by half.

Add the herbs, toss with the pasta and serve with Romano cheese. Serves 4.

Serve with Louis M. Martini Sauvignon Blanc.

Louis M. Martini Winery

A cool, flavorful dish for a warm evening or a summer luncheon.

Italian Rice Torta

2 cups cooked rice
4 eggs
2 heaping tablespoons pesto
 (finely chopped basil & parsley)

2 cloves garlic, finely chopped
1/2 cup Parmesan cheese
1/2 cup white wine
Salt and pepper to taste

Combine ingredients and bake 30 to 40 minutes at 350 degrees. For variations, add 1 cup chopped and cooked green onions or leeks, broccoli, French cut green beans or celery. Serves 6 to 8.

**Roselee Demonstene and Cindy Martin, Co-Owners
Sausal Winery**

Santa Clara Rice Dressing

1 cup short grain brown rice
2 cups chicken stock
1 cup Riesling or Chenin Blanc
1 teaspoon salt
3 tablespoons butter
4 ounces dried apricots, slivered
 (about 3/4 cup)
4 ounces pitted prunes, quartered

1 cup chopped celery
1 cup chopped onion
2 teaspoons dried sweet basil,
 crumbled
1/2 teaspoon thyme, crumbled
3/4 cup coarsely chopped
 walnuts, lightly toasted
1/4 cup chopped parsley

In a 3-quart saucepan with tight-fitting lid, combine rice, chicken stock, 1/2 cup of the wine, salt and 1 tablespoon butter. Bring to a boil. Lower heat until liquid is just simmering. Cover and simmer about 1 hour without removing lid. When liquid has evaporated, remove from heat and allow to steam, covered, for 10 to 15 minutes. Fluff rice with fork.

Meanwhile, place apricots in small pot. Top with prunes and 1/2 cup of the wine, and bring to a boil. Remove from heat and set aside to cool. Melt 2 tablespoons of the butter in skillet. Add celery, onions, basil and thyme. Saute over medium heat for 5 minutes. Add to rice, along with cooled fruits, walnuts and parsley. Toss well to combine. Spoon into buttered baking dish, cover, and heat in 325 degree oven for 30 minutes before serving. Serves 8.

Serve with Mirassou Monterey Riesling or Chenin Blanc.

Mirassou

A delicious rice dish, equally good with poultry or pork.

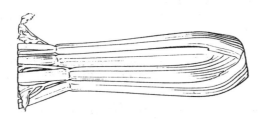

Meats

SPICES OF THE WORLD

Herb Marinated Lamb Chops

4 lamb chops, well trimmed
1/3 cup dry red wine
2 tablespoons spicy mustard
Juice of 2 tangerines
1/2 teaspoon salt
1 tablespoon cracked black
  pepper

2 tablespoons minced chives
1 teaspoon fresh rosemary,
  chopped
1 teaspoon fresh thyme,
  chopped
1/2 teaspoon red pepper
  flakes

Place lamb chops in a heavy dish. Mix remaining ingredients and pour over lamb, turning to coat. Marinate at room temperature at least one hour.

Broil or grill to desired doneness. (Medium-rare works best for us.) Serve on hot plates with asparagus, green beans or broccoli.

What else goes so well with Spring lamb, mustard and fresh herbs than a good Cabernet? Open a bottle of 1987 Napa Valley Cabernet Sauvignon, use a little in the marinade, maybe have a small glass while preparing the meal and there will be just enough left for a cozy dinner for two...

Robert O'Malley, Operations Manager
V. Sattui Winery

Robert O'Malley began his food career in San Francisco's North Beach restaurants in the early 1970's, working first as a waiter, than captain and Maitre d'. After a year's hiatus to travel, he became restaurant manager at The Stanford Court Hotel on Nob Hill, where he worked with chefs Larry Vito and Jim Dodge during that hotel's prominent period.

Simultaneously, he ran a successful small business, Robert O'Malley Catering, which provided him with a large number of proven recipes.

In 1989, Robert and his wife Michele, moved to the Napa Valley, where he now oversees wine and food operations at V. Sattui Winery in St. Helena.

Braised Beef Ragout with Sage Papardelle and Roasted Garlic Cabernet Sauce

MARINADE:

4 pounds beef (rump or round steak)
1 bay leaf
4 sprigs thyme
6 peppercorns
4 garlic cloves
2 shallots, sliced
2 whole cloves

1 large carrot, sliced
2 medium onions, sliced
1/2 of one rib celery stalk, sliced
2 parsley stems
6 cups Cabernet Sauvignon
1 cup vinegar

Cut the beef into 2-inch cubes. Divide vegetables and herbs into 2 parts, place half on the bottom of a stainless steel container, then the beef, followed by the other half. Pour wine and the vinegar over to cover. Leave refrigerated for 12 hours, turning the meat a couple of times.

BRAISING:

4 ounces pork rind (trimmed of all fat and blanched)
3 cups good brown stock
Small bouquet garni

2 tablespoons mashed roasted garlic
Oil
Salt and pepper

Remove beef from marinade and pat dry, reserve the marinade. Sear the beef in oil on top of the stove until a caramelized crust of juices has formed. Set the pieces of meat aside. When this has been done, strain the vegetables and herbs from the marinade, keeping the liquid. Saute the vegetables in the same pan as the beef, then pour in the liquid from the marinade and reduce by 2/3, releasing the sediments from the bottom of the pan with a wooden spoon.

When this is done, pour into a thick pot just big enough to hold the ingredients. There should be no large spaces between the meat and lid. Place the pork rind on the vegetables and add the pieces of beef. Barely cover the meat with the brown stock and bring to a boil. Add the bouquet garni and season with salt and pepper. Cover pot with foil leaving no gaps between meat and foil. Cover with pot lid. Braise in a 325 degree oven for 1 1/2 to 2 hours.

Remove pieces of beef to a clean pot; the stock should have reduced to a good consistency while cooking; if not, and remains somewhat thin, reduce it quickly until it reaches a nice coating on the back of a spoon. Strain over the beef adding the mashed roasted garlic, and correct the seasoning. At this point you may add some blanched baby vegetables, i.e., carrots, turnips, pearl onions, etc., or a mixture of sauteed wild mushrooms.

SAGE PAPARDELLE NOODLES:

1/2 cup sage leaves	1 teaspoon salt
1 whole egg (at room temperature)	1 1/4 cups unbleached all
2 egg yolks (at room temperature)	purpose flour

Blend eggs and yolks in a blender with the sage leaves. Sieve flour and salt into a table top. Make a well in the center adding about 80% of the egg and sage mixture to the well. In a circular motion with your fingertips, gradually incorporate the flour into the egg mixture. When a paste is formed, you may push most of the flour over the paste leaving any you may think you won't need. With both hands, knead the dough into a crumbly mass. If too dry, place a little egg mixture into the palm of your hand and carry on kneading. Knead the dough for about 12 minutes, so your dough is able to stretch without difficulty. Always rest the dough covered for about 30 minutes before cutting the dough following the instructions for your machine.

The Papardelle noodles should be approximately 1 by 3 1/2 inches. Cook in boiling salted water, approximately 3 minutes until tender and toss in seasoned olive oil before placing onto a serving platter under the braised beef.   Serves 6 to 8.

Serve with Chateau Souverain 1989 Alexander Valley Cabernet Sauvignon.

Martin W. Courtman, Executive Chef
Chateau Souverain

Grilled Steak Provencal

4 steaks, 6 to 8 ounce filets (filet mignon or New York)
2 tablespoons olive oil
2 large cloves garlic, minced
1 medium onion, thinly sliced
1/3 cup Cabernet Sauvignon, Merlot or Zinfandel
1/2 cup chicken broth

1 cup fresh tomatoes, chopped
1/2 cup Greek style olives, pitted and thinly sliced
1/2 teaspoon dried rosemary, crumbled
1/2 teaspoon dried oregano
Salt and pepper to taste

Start your grill. Rub both sides of each steak with 1 tablespoon oil, then sprinkle with salt and pepper. Grill steaks to desired doneness. Meanwhile, heat 1 tablespoon oil in a heavy skillet over medium-high heat; add garlic and onions. Saute until onions are tender, then add remaining ingredients. Increase heat under skillet to high; boil sauce until slightly thickened. Adjust seasonings. Spoon sauce over each steak.   Serves 4.

Outstanding with Dry Creek Vineyard Cabernet Sauvignon, Merlot or Zinfandel.

Brad Wallace
for
Dry Creek Vineyard

Nov 5, 1997

Mushroom Beef Stew

2+ → 2 pounds boneless beef chuck, cut
into 1 1/2-inch cubes
2 medium onions, sliced thin
2 clove garlic, minced
1 cup beef stock or canned broth
Flour
+ 2 cups dry red wine
3 tablespoons chopped fresh
parsley
1 1/2 teaspoons oregano
1/2 teaspoon thyme

1 bay leaf
3 tablespoons olive or other
vegetable oil
2 slices bacon, chopped
2 fresh tomatoes, chopped
1 pound mushrooms, cut in
thick slices
2 tablespoons butter
Salt and pepper to taste
Fresh parsley for garnish

Preheat oven to 325 degrees. Heat 3 tablespoon oil in heavy, large Dutch oven over high heat. Place flour on plate, season with salt and pepper. Coat beef with flour, shaking off excess. Brown beef a little at a time, browning well on all sides.

Return beef and any accumulated juices to Dutch oven. Reduce heat to medium. Add garlic and onion, and cook 1 minute. Add wine and enough beef stock to cover meat. Add parsley, oregano, thyme, and bay leaf. Cover and bake in oven about 2 hours.

Heat frying pan and cook bacon until crisp. Transfer to paper towel to drain. Add chopped tomatoes to pan and saute 5 minutes. Add bacon and tomatoes to stew. Thin liquid with wine, if necessary. Cover and bake approximately 30 minutes or until meat is tender.

Saute mushrooms in butter until tender. Add to stew just before serving. Season with salt and pepper to taste.   Serves 4 to 6.

Serve with Conn Creek Cabernet Sauvignon.

Conn Creek Winery

Estofado
Mediterranean Stew

2 large thinly sliced onions
1/4 cup olive oil
3 pounds very lean stew meat (tri-tip or sirloin)
1 bay leaf
2 tablespoons dried currants
6 ounces tomato paste
1/2 cup Zinfandel or dry red table wine
2 tablespoons wine vinegar

1 tablespoon brown sugar
1 large clove of garlic, minced or pressed
1/4 teaspoon ground cinnamon
1/2 teaspoon ground cumin
1/8 teaspoon ground cloves
1/2 pound Feta cheese
3/4-1 cup walnut halves
Salt and pepper

Cut meat into 1 1/2-inch cubes. Heat oil in a large frying pan until hot. Brown meat on all sides for 5 minutes on high heat. Stir to avoid sticking or scorching. Add onions and garlic and continue stirring for 5 minutes, until coated with oil. Add remaining ingredients except cheese and walnuts. Cover, reduce heat to low and simmer for 2 hours, until meat is tender and sauce is thick. Stir occasionally to prevent sticking. Just before serving, stir in cheese and walnuts. Serve with rice or noodles. Serves 6 to 8.

Suggested Wine: Granite Springs Cabernet Sauvignon or Petit Sirah.

Lynne Russell
Granite Springs Winery

Wente Chili

6 pounds top sirloin, trimmed and
cubed into 1/2-inch pieces
2 jalapenos, diced, no seeds
1 1/2 tablespoons chopped garlic
15 pear tomatoes, peeled and
seeded, or 1 #10 can (13 cups)
peeled tomatoes with juice

1 1/2 large onions, chopped
1 bottle Cabernet Sauvignon
1 quart chicken stock
5 chipolte peppers, diced
Salt and pepper
1 cup olive oil
2 cups fresh corn

SPICE MIX:

2 tablespoons chili powder
2 tablespoons paprika
1 tablespoon cumin

1 tablespoon cayenne
1 tablespoon coriander

Salt and pepper the beef. Heat 1 ounce of oil at a time in a thick-
bottomed stock pot. Brown off the beef in 3 batches, using more olive
oil each time. Add more oil (2 ounces), the onions and jalapenos.
Lightly brown the onions. Add the spice mixture and lower the heat.
Cook, stirring, for about 3 to 4 minutes. Add the wine, stock, tomatoes
and beef. Simmer until beef is tender, approximately 2 to 3 hours. Skim
the top regularly. Garnish with corn (2 cups). Serve with spoon bread
and lime cilantro créme frâiche.   Makes one gallon.

P.S. Next day, season with more paprika, chili powder and cayenne
to taste and heat!!!

Wine suggestion: A hearty full-bodied Wente Zinfandel or Cabernet.

Kimball Jones, Executive Chef
Wente Bros. Wine Cellars and Restaurant

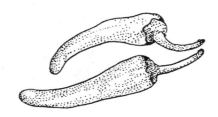

Grilled Flank Steak with
Red Wine and Shallot Sauce

Flank steak
Soy sauce

Ground pepper
1 tablespoon thyme

SAUCE:

1 cup chopped shallots or green
  onions
1/2 cup red wine
4 tablespoons butter

Salt to taste
1 tablespoon finely chopped
  parsley

Brush flank steak with soy sauce, freshly ground pepper and a teaspoon of dried thyme. Let stand for an hour or so. Brush again with soy sauce, pepper and thyme, and broil or grill 3 to 4 minutes on each side for rare steaks. Carve with sharp knife in thin slices on the diagonal.

For the sauce, combine shallots and red wine. Bring just to the boiling point. Add the butter and salt to taste. Stir until butter is melted. Add chopped parsley and spoon over the steak slices.

Serve with Louis M. Martini Cabernet Sauvignon.

Louis M. Martini Winery

Spicy Plum Pork

2 pounds pork shoulder, trimmed
and cut into 2-inch cubes
2 cups dry red wine, such as
Merlot
1 1/2 cups homemade plum
compote, or 1 16-ounce can
plums, including juice, plums
diced
10 dried apricots, diced
1 teaspoon allspice

3 cloves
1 bay leaf
1/2 teaspoon freshly grated
nutmeg
1/4 teaspoon cinnamon
1/4 teaspoon cayenne pepper
2-inch piece fresh ginger,
minced
3 cloves garlic, minced

Dredge the meat in seasoned flour and sear in hot oil in a large heavy Dutch oven. Add the remaining ingredients and bring to a simmer. Cover and place in a 350 degree oven for 2 hours.

Serve with basmati rice and roasted carrots.   Serves 4.

"This was always a delicious way for us to use my mothers freshly canned Santa Rosa plums in the winter months."

Serve with Monterey Vineyard Classic Merlot.

Elaine Bell, Culinary Director
Sterling Vineyards

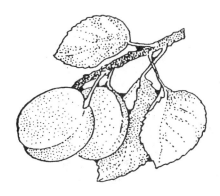

Basil Pork Chops Barbera

4 pork chops, center cut 1-inch thick	1/2 cup Barbera wine
3 tablespoons olive oil	1/4 cup fresh basil, chopped
8 large cloves garlic, chopped	1/4 cup fresh parsley, chopped
1 cup sliced green onions	Salt and freshly ground
8 ounces fresh mushrooms, sliced	pepper to taste
1 28-ounce can plum tomatoes, drained and crushed (reserve juice)	

In a heavy skillet, heat oil to medium temperature. Score edges of chops to prevent curling. Quickly brown chops on both sides. Remove to plate and set aside. Lower heat, add sliced mushrooms, green onions, basil, salt and pepper. Mix and saute for 2 minutes. Add chopped garlic and wine to deglaze pan. Add crushed tomatoes and mix well. Return chops with accumulated juice to skillet and spoon sauce over. Simmer uncovered for 45 minutes and sauce is reduced. Add reserved tomato liquid as needed to adjust sauce. Add chopped parsley 5 minutes before cooking time is completed.   Serves 4.

Serve with Round Hill 1991 Merlot California Appellation or Round Hill Napa Valley Zinfandel.

Charles Abela, President
Round Hill Vineyards

Baked Cranberry Pork Chops

4 loin pork chops (1 1/2 to 2 pounds)
1 medium onion sliced fine
1 can (16 ounces) jellied cranberry sauce
3 tablespoons water
2 tablespoons light brown sugar
1 teaspoon ground ginger
1/16 teaspoon ground nutmeg
2 cups fresh carrots cut in thin strips (julienned)
1 teaspoon cornstarch
1 tablespoon fresh chopped parsley
1 tablespoon vegetable oil

Brown pork chops in small amount of oil with sliced onion. Set aside. Preheat oven to 375 degrees.

In a medium saucepan, heat cranberry sauce, 2 tablespoons of water, brown sugar, ginger and nutmeg until cranberry sauce is melted, about 2 minutes. Place carrots in a 2 1/2-quart casserole. Arrange pork chops over carrots. Spoon cranberry sauce mixture evenly over pork chops. Cover and bake until pork is thoroughly cooked, about 45 minutes to 1 hour.

Remove chops to a serving plate. Scatter carrots over chops. Pour sauce remaining in casserole into a medium saucepan. Combine cornstarch with 1 tablespoon water; stir into saucepan. Cook and stir until sauce is clear and thickened, about 2 minutes. Spoon over pork chops. Sprinkle with chopped parsley.   Serves 4.

Serve with Sutter Home Zinfandel.

Sutter Home Winery

Nutmeg/Mace

Minted Grilled Lamb

1 leg of lamb (about 5 pounds) boned and butterflied, or 6 to 8 lamb steaks, cut 3/4 to 1-inch thick

1/2 cup firmly-packed parsley sprigs
1/2 cup firmly-packed fresh mint leaves
4 large cloves garlic, peeled and halved
4 green onions (including tops) cut into 1-inch pieces
2 tablespoons fresh lemon juice

2 tablespoons raspberry vinegar or red wine vinegar
1/2 teaspoon dried thyme, crushed
1/4 teaspoon dried rosemary, crushed
1/4 teaspoon pepper
1/3 cup olive oil

Place parsley, mint, garlic, green onions, lemon juice, vinegar, thyme, rosemary and pepper in a food processor or blender. Process until finely chopped. With motor running, slowly add olive oil to make a smooth paste. Rub marinade on all sides of lamb. Place lamb in a bowl, cover and refrigerate for 2 hours or overnight.

To cook, place lamb on a lightly greased grill, about 4 inches above a solid bed of low-glowing coals. Cook, turning occasionally, until lamb is well browned, but still pink in the center when cut. Allow about 50 minutes for leg, 12 to 15 minutes for steaks.

Makes 6 to 8 servings.

Serve with Montevina Cabernet Sauvignon.

Montevina Winery

Mint

Roast Leg of Lamb with Pesto Filling

1 5 to 6-pound leg of lamb, boned and butterflied	2 teaspoons dried rosemary
3/4 cup olive oil	1 teaspoon salt
2 cups firmly packed basil	1/2 teaspoon pepper
2 teaspoons minced garlic	1 cup fresh bread crumbs
	1/4 cup pine nuts

Preheat oven to 425 degrees. In a food processor, blend the olive oil, basil, garlic, rosemary, salt, and pepper until well blended. Reserve 2 teaspoons of the mixture. Add next the bread crumbs, then the pine nuts to the food processor. Process until just blended. Spread the filling evenly over the lamb. Roll the lamb, tucking in the ends and tie securely with string. Rub the outside with the reserved pesto.

Place lamb in shallow roasting pan and roast for 1 hour for rare meat (12 minutes per pound, 135 degrees on a meat thermometer; for medium, allow 15 minutes per pound, about 150 degrees on meat thermometer).

Allow lamb to rest 15 minutes before carving (internal temperature will rise 5 to 10 degrees). Cut into 1/2-inch thick slices and serve.

Serves 8 to 10.

Serve with Benziger Family Sonoma County Merlot.

Stella Fleming, Executive Chef
Benziger Family Winery

119

Lamb with Cilantro/Cumin Crust

2 whole lamb loins
Olive oil
1/2 bunch cilantro, stems removed

2 tablespoons ground cumin
1/2 teaspoon cayenne pepper
Salt to taste

Clean the loins of all fat and silverskin. If the tenderloins are attached, clean them as well. Brush with olive oil and sprinkle with salt.

Puree the cilantro leaves in a food processor with the cumin and cayenne. Add olive oil a tablespoon at a time until mixture is the consistency of jam. Smear over the loins and set aside, covered, for 1/2 to 1 hour. (They may also be held overnight, refrigerated.)

Prepare a charcoal fire or preheat a gas grill.

Grill the loins for approximately 4 minutes per side for rare. (Times are approximate due to the variability of grill temperatures.) Meat should spring back to the touch -- or, use the sharp point of a knife to test for desired doneness. The smaller tenderloins will, of course, cook more quickly.

Let meat rest for a few minutes, then cut into slices and arrange on warmed plates.   Serves 4.

Serve with Simi Sauvignon Blanc Wine.

Mary Evely, Chef
Simi Winery

Spicy Tangine of Lamb with Apples

3 to 3 1/2 pounds shoulder of
lamb or beef chuck in 1 1/2-inch
cubes
2 tablespoons sweet butter, melted
2 tablespoons vegetable oil
Pinch of saffron
Salt and pepper to taste

1 scant teaspoon ground
ginger
1/4 teaspoon cinnamon
3 tablespoons grated onion
4-5 sprigs coriander, tied
together

Mix last 6 ingredients with butter and oil. Dip each chunk of meat in
butter mixture and place in casserole. Over gentle heat turn pieces,
being careful not to burn and allowing aroma of spices to be released.
Cover with water, bring to boil, then lower heat. Simmer 1 hour.

1 pound dried pitted prunes or
apricots
1 cup finely sliced onions
1/4 teaspoon cinnamon
3 tablespoons honey
4 tart apples

1 tablespoon butter
1 tablespoon honey
1/4 teaspoon cinnamon
1 tablespoon toasted sesame
seeds

Meanwhile, soak prunes in 2 cups cold water. After one hour, add
prunes, the cup of sliced onions, the 1/4 teaspoon cinnamon and the
honey to meat. Simmer uncovered until prunes swell and sauce has
reduced to one cup.

Shortly before ready to serve, quarter and core apples. Saute in skillet
with honey, cinnamon and butter until soft and glazed.

To serve, arrange meat on dish, pour onion-prune sauce over, decorate
with apples and sprinkle with toasted sesame seeds. Nice served with
cous cous or rice.   Serves 8.

Serve with Quivira Vineyards Cabernet or Zinfandel.

Holly P. Wendt, Proprietor
Quivira Vineyards

Mirassou Vintner's Stew

4 ounces bacon, chopped (4-5 slices)
2 large onions, coarsely chopped (about 3 cups)
4-6 tablespoons olive oil
1/2 cup flour
1 teaspoon salt
1 teaspoon freshly ground pepper
3 pounds chuck or cross rib beef, cut into 2-inch cubes
1 1/2 cups Cabernet Sauvignon
1 cup beef broth
1 8-ounce can tomato sauce

1 large bay leaf
1/2 teaspoon dried thyme, crumbled
2 large garlic cloves, minced
1 tablespoon Worcestershire sauce
1/2 ounce unsweetened chocolate, chopped
18 boiling onions, peeled
1 1/2 pounds carrots, peeled and cut into 2-inch lengths
3/4 pound small fresh mushrooms

In a heavy pot (6-7 quarts) with tight-fitting lid, saute bacon until all fat is rendered. Remove crisp bacon bits. Cook chopped onion in bacon fat over medium-high heat, stirring often, until dark brown but not burnt, at least 30 minutes. Remove onions and add 2 tablespoons of oil to the pot. Place flour, salt and pepper in small bag. Add beef cubes a few at a time and shake to coat well. Brown meat in small batches (don't crowd the pot), adding more oil as needed. Transfer meat to bowl after browning. Add wine and broth to pot. Bring to a boil over high heat, scraping up any brown bits on bottom and sides of pot. Add tomato sauce, bay leaf, thyme, garlic, Worcestershire sauce, bacon bits, browned onions and meat. Stir well and return to a boil. Lower heat, cover tightly and simmer 30 minutes. Stir every 15 minutes throughout 1 1/2 hours of cooking time. Add chocolate, stirring until dissolved. Stir in small onions, cover and simmer 30 minutes. Add carrots and mushrooms. Cover and cook for another 30 minutes.

Serve with boiled red-skinned potatoes (unpeeled) tossed with chopped parsley, a crisp green salad and Mirassou Cabernet Sauvignon.

Serving Suggestion: Serve in individual round French bread loaves. Slice top from each small loaf and hollow out the center, leaving a 3/4-inch thick shell. Spoon stew into bread shells. Replace tops, slightly off center.   Serves 6.

Mirassou

Carneros Lamb

3-pound leg of lamb
1 cup Pinot Noir
1 cup light soy sauce
1/2 cup olive oil
1/4 cup coarse mustard
Zest of lemon

Handful of rosemary
Handful of oregano
Handful of mint
1 tablespoon cracked pepper
1 teaspoon sea salt

Have the butcher butterfly a leg of lamb, making sure that the thickest parts are not more than 2 inches thick. If using fresh herbs, coarsely chop (or cut the herbs with scissors) into 1-inch chunks. Put the ingredients of the marinade in a large bowl. Place the lamb in the bowl fat side up, so that the meat is in contact with the juices. Refrigerate; marinate for at least 4 hours, preferably overnight.

Strain and reserve the marinade. Reduce over high heat while the lamb is cooking. Grill the lamb over a hot fire, turning several times, until done, but still pink. Let rest 15 minutes before carving. Add any meat juices to the reduced marinade. Serve lamb with mixed grilled vegetables, black pepper pasta with caramelized onions, and a reduced Pinot Noir Herb Sauce.   Serves 4 to 6.

Serve with Buena Vista Carneros Pinot Noir.

Buena Vista Carneros Estate

Braised Rabbit with Sweet Potatoes, Lentils, and Meyer Lemon, Garlic and Green Beans

1 rabbit
3 tablespoons peanut oil
1 large onion, quartered
1 carrot, cut in half
1 head garlic, cut in half
3 stalks celery
Several large sprigs rosemary

3 branches sage
3 branches thyme
2 cups Fumé Blanc
2-3 cups water
Salt and freshly ground
　pepper to taste

TO PREPARE RABBIT:
Cut rabbit into 8 pieces. Salt and sear in small amount of peanut oil until well browned. Pour off oil, return rabbit to pan and add quartered onion, carrot, garlic, 3 whole stalks of celery, fresh sprigs of rosemary, sage and thyme. Add Fumé Blanc and water (just enough to barely cover rabbit). Simmer for about one hour.

VEGETABLES:
1 small sweet potato
1 small white onion, diced
1/2 pound lentils
3 cups vegetable stock
2 sprigs thyme

1 pound haricots verts, or
　young tender Blue Lake beans
2 Meyer lemons, quartered
1 head garlic, cut in half
1/4 cup extra virgin olive oil
Salt

TO PREPARE VEGETABLES:
Dice the small sweet potatoes and white onion, and rinse the lentils. Cook lentils in 3 times their volume of vegetable stock and water with sweet potatoes, onion and several sprigs of thyme for about 30 minutes. Season to taste with salt. Snip off stem ends of green beans leaving the tips natural. Blanch several minutes in boiling water, then refresh with ice water to set and retain their bright green color. Finish just before serving with olive oil and head of garlic (cut in half) and quartered Meyer lemons. Season with salt to taste.

TO FINISH:
Remove rabbit from cooking liquid, strain and pour sauce back over the rabbit (you can reduce it a bit first if you like). Serve rabbit and natural sauce over the lentils, garnish with green beans with a cooked Meyer lemon wedge and a rosemary or sage garnish.　　Serves 6.

Enjoy with Robert Mondavi Cabernet Sauvignon.

Note: One of the leanest and healthiest meats is rabbit, so this is particularly good for you. All of the ingredients (lentils, garlic, green beans, herbs) contribute to good health. H.P.

Holly Peterson, Head Chef
Wine and Food Education
Robert Mondavi Winery

Holly Peterson, Head Chef/Wine and Food Education of Robert Mondavi Winery since 1985, had a distinguished career in Europe prior to joining the winery. A graduate, in Science, of the University of California at Davis, she also has a Grand Diplome de Cuisine from Ecole de Cuisine La Varenne in Paris. She interned in La Truffiere Restaurant in Paris, in sensory evaluation at chateau Mouton Rothschild, and enological programs at Krug and Remy Martin. She travels extensively, teaching food and wine pairings to chefs throughout the world.

Fricassee of Rabbit with Wild Mushrooms

1 rabbit, cut into eight pieces
1 tablespoon fresh thyme leaves
Salt and freshly ground black
 pepper (to taste)
Olive oil, as needed
3 tablespoons Brandy
2 large cloves garlic, minced
2 bay leaves
1/2 cup Chardonnay

1 cup reduced veal stock, or
 low-salt canned chicken broth
1 cup creme frâiche or heavy
 whipping cream
1 pound wild mushrooms,
 sliced
Unsalted butter, as needed
2 tablespoons chopped Italian
 parsley

Sprinkle rabbit with thyme, salt and pepper, and saute in hot oil until golden brown. Remove rabbit from pan and pour off oil.

Return rabbit to pan. Add brandy, stand back, and ignite! When flames die down, add garlic, bay leaves, wine, stock and creme frâiche. Simmer, covered, for approximately 1 hour, or until rabbit is very tender.

While the rabbit is cooking, saute the mushrooms in a little butter. Add to the rabbit during the last 10 minutes of cooking. Arrange the fricassee on a platter and garnish with chopped parsley. Serves 4.

Suggested wine: Rodney Strong Vineyards Chalk Hill Chardonnay.

Bea Beasley
for
Rodney Strong Vineyards

Butterflied Leg of Lamb

1 butterflied leg of lamb (about 4 to 5 pounds with the bone out). (Have your friendly butcher butterfly it for you.)

2/3 cup Shoyu Sauce (or low salt soy sauce)
1 tablespoon Herbs de Provence *

Combine the Shoyu Sauce and Herbs de Provence. Place the lamb in a glass dish and pour marinade over it. Place in the refrigerator for twelve hours, turning the lamb from time to time to ensure it is well marinated. (It may be left as long as 24 hours.)

Remove the lamb from the refrigerator approximately 1 hour before grilling.

Drain the lamb, but save the marinade.

Prepare mesquite coals (combine with grapevine or applewood cuttings if they are available).

Grill the lamb approximately 5 inches from the coals for 20 minutes per side. Baste frequently with marinade.

When done, remove onto a warm plate and let stand 10 minutes prior to serving.

Serve with your favorite red potato, pasta or rice salad.   Serves 8.

* *An aromatic blend of thyme, summer savory, basil, rosemary and lavender.*

Recommended wine: 1991 Merryvale Vineyards Napa Valley Merlot.

Robert Levy, Winemaker
Merryvale Vineyards

Roasted Rack of Lamb with
Cabernet Rosemary Tangerine Sauce

1 crown lamb rack, frenched and trimmed (about 8 chops)
4 cloves garlic, coarsely chopped
2 tablespoons each of finely chopped fresh rosemary, thyme, parsley, mint and basil
2 tablespoons olive oil
Salt and pepper to taste
1/4 cup Brandy
1 tablespoon tangerine zest
1 tablespoon Dijon mustard

Rub lamb with salt and pepper, herbs, tangerine zest and mustard. Let set overnight, or at least 6 hours. Sear lamb in olive oil, meat side down, until golden brown. Deglaze with Brandy. Add garlic and turn rack over until it rests on bones. Roast in oven until rare (450 degrees for about 20 to 30 minutes).

TANGERINE SAUCE:

1/2 cup honey
2 tablespoons mint, finely chopped
1/4 cup Dijon mustard
1/4 cup grain mustard
Additional tangerine zest
1/2 cup Cabernet Sauvignon
2 ounces rich lamb stock (or beef stock)
Salt and pepper to taste
1 tablespoon butter, cut into pieces
Fresh rosemary to garnish

While meat is roasting, make the tangerine sauce by mixing all ingredients together except for wine and lamb stock. When lamb is ready, remove from pan and pour off excess grease. Deglaze with Cabernet, let reduce, add lamb stock and again reduce down. Add the tangerine sauce and stir thoroughly, adding pieces of butter until smooth. Keep warm. Arrange lamb chops on prepared dish and drizzle sauce over lamb. Garnish with fresh rosemary and tangerine rind twists.

Accompany with oven-braised fennel or fennel puree.   Serves 4.

Serve with Ferrari-Carano Alexander Valley Cabernet Sauvignon.

Rhonda Carano, Co-Owner
Ferrari-Carano Vineyards & Winery

Seafood

SPICES OF THE WORLD

Herb Baked Salmon
with Lemon Thyme Cream Sauce

4 salmon fillets (approximately 6 ounces each)
1/2 pound fresh lobster meat
1 tablespoon thyme, chopped
1 tablespoon cilantro, chopped
1 tablespoon basil, chopped

1 tablespoon lemon balm, chopped
1/4 cup white wine
Salt and pepper
Butter

Note: Use fresh herbs, if available.

LEMON THYME CREAM SAUCE:

1/2 cup white wine
1/2 cup fish stock
1 teaspoon lemon thyme (chopped)

4 teaspoons lemon juice
1 chopped shallot
1/2 cup cream
Salt and pepper (to taste)

Place salmon on greased pan. Splash with wine and dust with chopped herbs. Dot with small amount of butter. Bake at 375 degrees for 10 to 15 minutes. Check while cooking. Fish should not be overcooked.

For Lemon Thyme Cream Sauce, combine all ingredients, except cream and seasonings, in sauce pan. Reduce liquid by 1/3 by boiling. Add cream and lobster meat, simmering until lobster is warm and sauce is correct consistency. Season with salt and pepper to taste.

Serve salmon topped with sauce and a sprig of fresh lemon thyme.
Serves 4.

Serve with Sutter Home 1991 California Chardonnay.

Sutter Home Winery

Risotto with Grilled Fennel and
Chateau Cured Salmon

6 ounces center-cut salmon
1/2 ounce Kosher salt
1 ounce sugar
3 tablespoons chopped dill
Ground pepper
Olive oil
5 cups fish stock
5 tablespoons butter

1 1/2 cups Arborio rice
1/2 cup Parmesan cheese
1/2 medium onion, chopped
1/2 cup Chardonnay
Salt and pepper
1 fennel bulb
1/2 teaspoon toasted and
  ground fennel seeds

The salmon needs at least 3 days for preparation. Simply mix the salt and sugar together, lay the salmon, skin-side down, on some clear wrap, pack the salt and sugar mixture on the salmon, and wrap the salmon tightly with the clear wrap, then in foil. Place on a plate in the refrigerator with about a pound weight on top. After 2 days, open and place some fresh ground pepper, 2 teaspoons olive oil, and the chopped dill on top. Re-wrap, and return to the refrigerator with the weight on top. After the third day, the salmon may be sliced as needed.

Put the fish stock in a sauce pan to simmer. Melt the butter and saute the onions. Add the fennel seeds and Arborio rice, and stir for 2 minutes. Add the wine and reduce to medium heat. The stock should be added 1/2 cup at a time. Don't drown the rice. Attention should be paid to the heat -- if the stock is reduced too fast, the risotto ends up soft on the outside and chalky in the middle. If reduced to slowly, it becomes gluey. The risotto should stop cooking when it is al dente (about 20 minutes). Also, the liquid you add may vary from time to time. Season the finished risotto and add the Parmesan. (For a slightly richer risotto, add 4 ounces of reduced cream.)

The fennel bulb should be sliced with the root holding the slice together. Brush with olive oil and grill until cooked. Then, cut out the root, leaving just enough to keep the slice together.

The risotto is placed in the middle of the plate (a small ring about 4 inches wide may be used to make a neat presentation). Place the grilled fennel slice on top and about three thin slices of the Chateau Cured Salmon around the side. Garnish with a sprig of fresh dill or fennel top.   Serves 8 to 12.

Recommended Wine: Chateau Souverain Chardonnay.

Martin W. Courtman, Executive Chef
Chateau Souverain

Martin W. Courtman, Executive Chef at Chateau Souverain, a native of England, received his schooling, first at Harlow College, and then from the City and Guilds of London Institute's Certification Program in Food Preparation, Service, Catering and Beverages, with honors.

His restaurant experience in the United States includes key positions at The Mansion on Turtle Creek in Dallas, the Carlyle in Houston, and as Executive Chef of the Stanley Hotels in Estes Park, Colorado.

His cuisine features modern, yet simple foods, carefully matched to the wines of Chateau Souverain.

Salmon with Lavender

3 pounds fresh salmon, cut in 1-inch slices
2 tablespoons whole black peppercorns
2 tablespoons Szechuan peppercorns
2 tablespoons fresh, or 4 tablespoons dried lavender flowers and/or buds *

2 tablespoons olive oil
2 tablespoons butter
3 tablespoons minced shallots
1 cup chicken stock
1 cup Cabernet Sauvignon
4 tablespoons softened butter

Crush peppercorns with pestle or process with steel blade in food processor.

Mix pepper with lavender and press into both sides of the salmon slices. Cover and let stand at least 1/2 hour, up to 3 hours for maximum pepper flavor. Sear over high heat in butter and oil, 3 to 4 minutes on each side. (This is a dish that can be served rare.) Check for desired doneness by piercing with the point of a small, sharp knife.

Hold fish in a warm oven while making the sauce. Add shallots to saute pan and cook about one minute. Deglaze the pan with the stock, then add the Cabernet and cook rapidly until reduced by half. Remove pan from heat and stir in butter.

Pour sauce over salmon and serve immediately.   Serves 6.

*   Dried lavender is available in many health food stores.

Suggested wine: Simi Cabernet Sauvignon.

**Mary Evely, Chef
Simi Winery**

Spicy Hazelnut Salmon
with Peach Relish

4 salmon fillets (7 to 8 ounces each)
1 1/2 cup roasted, ground hazelnuts
1 teaspoon cayenne pepper

1/2 teaspoon thyme
1/2 teaspoon oregano
1 tablespoon oil
2 tablespoons butter

Mix ground nuts, pepper, thyme and oregano. Oil the salmon and "bread" it with the nut-herb mixture. Slightly brown in a frying pan with butter. Finish for 8 to 10 minutes in a 350 degree oven. Serve on peach relish.

PEACH RELISH:

4 peaches, peeled and cubed
1/2 cup red onions, chopped
1/2 cup white sugar
2 tablespoons raspberry vinegar

1 teaspoon chili powder
Salt and pepper
1 tablespoon oil

Put oil in pan, saute onions until soft, but not brown. Add peaches, sugar, vinegar and chili powder. Cook for 10 to 15 minutes. Season to taste.   Serves 4.

Serve with Kunde Estate Chardonnay.

Kunde Estate Winery

Oven-Roasted Salmon
with an Orange and Dill Beurre Blanc

4 5-ounce salmon filets (skin removed)
1 cup plus 3 tablespoons sweet unsalted butter
3 tablespoons light oil (olive or safflower)
1 cup sparkling wine

2 medium shallots, coarsely chopped
1/3 cup whipping cream
Zest of 1 orange
1/4 cup chopped fresh dill
Salt and freshly ground pepper to taste

The process of preparing this dish moves fairly quickly, so there are a few things to do ahead of time. First, go over the salmon carefully with your fingers to detect any little bones; pull them out with tweezers or pliers. Salt and pepper the fish and set aside in the refrigerator. You need to have your orange zested and also have your dill chopped. Cut your 1 cup butter into small pieces and refrigerate. Preheat oven to 450 degrees.

PREPARING THE BEURRE BLANC:

In a medium sauce pan, add the chopped shallots and sparkling wine and place on stove. Turn stove to medium-low heat. You will be reducing this mixture down to about 1/4 cup and this process will take about 15 minutes. Once it has reduced you can now add the cream. You will be reducing that mixture down by half. That will take about 7 to 10 minutes. Watch very closely, as it can very easily boil over. At this point, take this mixture off the heat and pour it into a blender. (I like to use a bar blender, but any kind will do.)

Take your cold, chopped butter out of the refrigerator and add to the hot wine mixture. Place a towel over the cover of the blender and hold your hand over that. At first, turn on to low power, then keep increasing to highest power until it is well blended. Turn off blender and add the orange zest, chopped dill, and salt and pepper to taste. Put sauce into a double boiler on low heat to keep warm.

PREPARING THE SALMON:

In a large skillet, melt the 3 tablespoons butter with the 3 tablespoons oil on low heat. Once the butter has melted, turn your heat up to high. It should take a little over a minute for the pan to become extremely hot, that is how you want it. Add the salmon and cook for 1 1/2 minutes on each side, or until golden brown. Then put into the oven and roast for 5 minutes. Remove from oven.

ASSEMBLING:

Place fish on to the left side of each plate and spoon sauce over the entire piece of fish. Garnish with an orange slice and a sprig of dill. I recommend that you serve this dish with wilted spinach or creamy mashed potatoes. Serves 4.

Serve with Domaine Carneros Sparkling Wine.

Trish Thomas, Chef
Domaine Carneros

The salmon has a crispy texture on the outside, and a very tender, succulent inside when paired with the creamy beurre blanc.

Salmon and Summer Squash Lasagna with Opal Basil and Chive Beurre Blanc

3 pounds salmon
1 bunch opal basil (can substitute
 regular basil)
3 sunburst squash

3 zucchini
1/2 pound Parmesan cheese
1 cup heavy cream
Salt and pepper

Take a whole side of salmon, weighing approximately 3 pounds. Slice the salmon in half lengthwise. Salt and pepper the salmon.

Pick all of the basil leaves from one bunch opal basil. Keep the prettiest for garnish. Wash 3 sunburst squash and 3 zucchini and slice as thin as possible. Keep separate. Grate 1/2 pound Parmesan cheese.

PASTA:

1 cup all-purpose flour
1/2 cup semolina

2 eggs
Pinch of salt

Mix the flours and salt together. Place on a work surface and make a well in the center of the flour. With a fork, whisk the eggs together and slowly incorporate the flour. Knead until together. If too dry, work a little cold water in. If too wet, add flour as you roll out. Roll out on a pasta machine to the thinnest setting. Cut to the length of your baking pan. Cook in boiling water for approximately 1 to 2 minutes. It should be al dente.

Pan should be approximately 12 X 9 1/2 X 2 inches. Cover the bottom of your baking pan with a light coating of cream. Place a layer of pasta on the bottom of the pan. Place a layer of the salmon on the pasta, sprinkle heavily with opal basil and sprinkle with cream. Place another layer of pasta over the salmon. Layer the squash and zucchini in this order: sunburst, salt and pepper, sprinkle with cheese, zucchini, salt and pepper, sprinkle with cream. Top with another layer of pasta, sprinkle with cream and the remaining cheese.

Bake in a 350 degree oven until the internal temperature is approximately 130 degrees on an instant-read thermometer, approximately 30 minutes. Let rest, and make your sauce.

CHIVE BEURRE BLANC:

1 cup white wine
1/2 cup white wine vinegar
1 shallot, diced
A few white peppercorns

1/2 cup cream
1/2 pound butter
1/4 bunch chives

Reduce the wine, vinegar, shallots and peppercorns to approximately 2 tablespoons. Add the cream and reduce by half, very slowly. Whisk in the butter. Chop the chives and add to the sauce.

Place the Chive Beurre Blanc on the bottom of each plate (about 1 ounce per plate). Cut the lasagna into 8 servings. Place on top of the sauce and garnish with a sprig of opal basil.   Serves 4.

Wine suggestion: Buttery, fruity Chardonnay.

Kimball Jones, Executive Chef
Wente Bros. Wine Cellars & Restaurant

Cilantro Cured Salmon

1 whole tail section of fresh
salmon, about 2 pounds
3 tablespoons coarse salt
2 tablespoons sugar
2 tablespoons ground pasilla (or
other mild) chili pepper

2 bunches fresh cilantro
2 medium or 1 large jicama
4 tablespoons lime juice
1 cup plain yogurt, lowfat or
nonfat (optional)

Have your fishmonger scale and butterfly fish, removing all bones (when finished, salmon should open like a book, with skin side out).

Mix salt, sugar and pasilla pepper together and rub over all surfaces of the fish.

Wash and coarsely chop one bunch of cilantro. Make a bed of 1/3 of the cilantro on a glass or ceramic dish that will fit the salmon.

Place salmon, skin side down, on the cilantro and distribute 1/3 on flesh. Fold fish back together and cover top with remaining cilantro. Cover securely with plastic wrap and weight the fish with a brick or an iron frying pan. Refrigerate for 48 to 72 hours, turning fish occasionally.

TO SERVE:

Peel jicama and cut in thin slices, about 1/8-inch thick. Cut into decorative shapes with a cookie cutter, if desired. Put in a shallow bowl and cover with lime juice. Wipe marinade off salmon. Cut on the bias into thin slices, detaching the slices from the skin as you go. Place pieces of salmon on jicama slices and top with fresh cilantro leaves.**

For optional sauce, mix 1/3 cup minced cilantro leaves with yogurt and place a small spoonful on each plate.

Serves 6 as first course, or 18 to 20 as an appetizer.

** For appetizer, cut into pieces approximately 1-inch square.

Serve with Simi Sauvignon Blanc.

Mary Evely, Chef
Simi Winery

Medallions of Salmon with Pine Nut Herb Crust

1 8-ounce fillet of salmon (center cut) skin removed
2 ounces pine nuts
3 ounces fine bread crumbs
5 ounces butter
2 tablespoons finely chopped shallots
1 tablespoon finely chopped chives
1 tablespoon finely chopped tarragon
1 tablespoon finely chopped thyme
Salt and pepper

Remove all small bones from the salmon fillet. Remove the grey area on the underside of the fillet. Place the salmon between two pieces of plastic wrap and lightly pound with flat side of a large knife until salmon fillet is an even thickness of approximately 1/2 to 3/4 of an inch. Season with salt and pepper. Roll salmon up in a sausage shape and wrap in a piece of plastic wrap, tying both ends tightly. Steam wrapped salmon approximately 3 minutes until it holds its shape. Cool before unwrapping. Set aside.

Toast pine nuts in oven and chop them finely in a food processor. Saute chopped shallots in melted butter for about 1 minute and add bread crumbs, pine nuts and chopped herbs. Season with salt and pepper, if necessary. Let cool.

Cut salmon roll in half. The center should be raw. Cut a small piece off each end of the salmon so it can stand upright. Press a small mound of pine nut mixture on top of each salmon medallion. Place medallion on an oiled sheet pan in a 400 degree oven for approximately 4 minutes. Serve with buerre blanc sauce. Serves 2.

Serve with Jordan Estate Bottled Chardonnay.

John Caputo, Chef de Cuisine
Jordan Vineyards and Winery

Shanghai Lobster Risotto with
Spicy Ginger and Julienne of Green Onions

1 piece fresh ginger (1 inch)
2 cloves garlic, minced
3/4 cup plum wine or Port
2 tablespoons rice wine vinegar
1 2-pound lobster, split lengthwise
2 tablespoons peanut oil
2 tablespoons unsalted butter
4 scallions, cut into 3/8-inch slices
1-2 teaspoons curry powder

1/4 cup dry white wine
1/2 cup fish stock
1/2 cup heavy cream
1/2 teaspoon dried hot chili
 flakes
1 tablespoon Chinese black
 vinegar or balsamic vinegar
Salt
Freshly ground pepper

Preheat oven to 500 degrees.

Peel the ginger, reserving the peels, and cut it into fine julienne strips. Cut the peels into coarse julienne strips and set aside.

In a small saucepan, cook the ginger and garlic with 1/2 cup of the plum wine and the rice wine vinegar until 1 tablespoon of liquid remains. Remove from the heat and reserve.

Place a heavy heatproof 12-inch skillet over high heat until it is very hot. Add the oil and heat it almost to the smoking point. Carefully add the lobster halves, meat side down. Cook 3 minutes. Turn the lobster over and add 1 tablespoon of the butter. Continue to saute until the lobster shells are getting red and the butter is nutty red. Transfer the lobster to the oven for about 10 minutes, or until the lobster is just cooked. Remove from the oven, remove the lobster from the skillet and keep warm.

Add the scallions, ginger peels and curry powder to the skillet. (Be careful the handle might be hot.) Saute the mixture lightly for 10 to 15 minutes, then whisk in the remaining plum wine and the white wine, fish stock, chili flakes and the vinegar. Reduce the liquid to 1/2 cup. Add the cream and reduce it by half. Add any liquid from the julienne of ginger, then whisk in the remaining tablespoon butter. Season the sauce to taste with salt and pepper.

Crack the lobster claws with the back of a large chef's knife.

PRESENTATION:

Arrange the lobster halves on a warm oval platter, meat side up. Strain the sauce over the lobster, then sprinkle with sweet ginger on top. Serve with Risotto.   Serves 2.

RISOTTO:

1 cup arborio rice
4 cups fish stock

Saute rice in butter, to coat well. Add 2 cups fish stock, bring to a boil. Then, turn to low heat to simmer, stirring and adding more stock as it is absorbed by the rice. Cook until tender, about 40 to 45 minutes.

Serve with Scharffenberger Cellars Blanc de Blanc, 1988.

Kazuto Matsusaka
for
Scharffenberger Cellars

Kazuto Matsusaka has been Executive Chef at Wolfgang Puck's famous restaurant "Chinois on Main" in Santa Monica for more than 5 years.

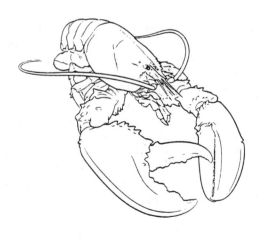

California Fish Soup

This is a very simple soup to make, yet it has a delicious flavor and is equally as good as a labor-intensive Marseilles Bouillabaisse. It is best to have two, or better yet, three kinds of fish for this dish. Ling cod, halibut and sea bass make a good combination of flavors. Use a good, flavorful, dry white wine, one that you would serve with it as well.

1/2 teaspoon saffron threads
3 tablespoons olive oil
3 cloves garlic, minced
1 medium onion, peeled and diced
1 leek, trimmed, washed and
sliced (white, with part of green)
1/2 cup diced celery
1/2 teaspoon paprika
3 medium potatoes, peeled and
cubed
3 medium tomatoes, peeled and
chopped
1 bay leaf

2-3 sprigs fresh thyme, or 1
teaspoon dried
3 sprigs parsley
2 strips fresh orange peel (1/2
inch wide by 2 inches long)
5 cups water
1 cup dry white wine
Sea salt and freshly ground
black pepper
2 1/2 pounds assorted fresh
white fish, such as halibut,
cod, bass, red snapper or
sole, cut into 2 inch pieces,
bones out

Place the saffron and a pinch of salt in a metal kitchen spoon. Hold over heat for a few seconds to get warm and, with a teaspoon, crush thread to a powder. Set aside.

Heat the olive oil in a large saucepan, add the garlic, onion, leek, celery and paprika. Cook gently for 2 to 3 minutes while stirring until onion is transparent. Add the cubed potatoes, tomatoes, bay leaf, thyme, parsley and orange peel. Cover and gently cook for 5 minutes. stirring occasionally.

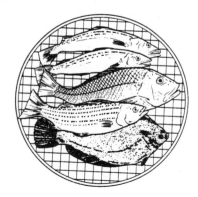

Add the prepared saffron, water, wine, sea salt and freshly ground pepper. Cover and simmer for 20 to 25 minutes. Add the fish, adding a little more water or wine if necessary. Cover and cook at a gentle simmer for 10 to 15 minutes until fish is just cooked through (depending on size of fish pieces). Do not overcook. Check seasonings, adding a dash of Cayenne pepper if desired. Serves 6.

Serve with French bread.

Chuck Williams
Williams Sonoma Company

Chuck Williams is best known as the Founder of the very, very successful Williams Sonoma Company, whose multi-million copy catalogues and their stores, cover the world today. To those of us in the California Wine Country, he is also highly respected as a gourmet cook, originally from Sonoma, where his quest for cooking utensils led to the founding of the firm that bears his name.

Scallop Saute with Leek and Allspice

FOR EACH PERSON:

5-6 ounces scallops
1 tablespoon butter, melted
An inch of white leek, cut in rings
 and separated
2 ounces Sauvignon Blanc or other
 soft dry wine

A pinch each of salt and
 allspice and a very sparing
 pinch of cayenne
2 tablespoons butter

Melt the butter in a pan large enough to hold all your scallops in a single layer. Add the scallops and leeks simultaneously, tossing or stirring gently over medium heat. Be careful, leeks burn more readily than other onions. When the scallops are opaque, but still spring back a little to the touch, pour on the wine and add the seasonings. When the wine simmers, remove the scallops with a slotted spoon to a heated serving dish or bed of rice.

Raise the heat to reduce the wine and scallop juices to a thick syrup. Remove the pan from the heat and swirl in the cool butter bit by bit, returning to low heat briefly as required. The butter will blend most easily if taken out of the refrigerator a half hour before it is needed. When all the butter has been incorporated, pour this sauce over the scallops.

NOTE: There is no such thing as a tough scallop. There are overcooked scallops, though even these are not so much tough as dry.

Chefs Robert Engel and Christine Topolos
Russian River Vineyards Restaurant

Allspice

Sauteed Medallions of Tuna with Papaya Chutney and Cilantro Pesto

FOR FISH:

12 medallions of tuna filets, 1 1/2 ounces each
2 tablespoons olive oil
Salt and white pepper

FOR PESTO:

1 cup chopped cilantro
3 cloves garlic
5 tablespoons olive oil
2 tablespoons finely chopped ginger

FOR CHUTNEY:

1 cup diced ripe papaya
1 tablespoon chopped mint leaves

2 tablespoons chopped scallions
2 tablespoons toasted pine nuts
Salt to taste

Combine all pesto ingredients in a food processor. Blend a few seconds until well mixed. Set aside at room temperature.

Mix together papaya and mint and set aside as well.

Heat olive oil in skillet. Season tuna and saute on both sides just until done, a minute or two at most.

Put the tuna on hot plates. Top with pesto. Spoon the chutney on the side. Serve immediately.   Serves 6.

Suggested wine: V. Sattui Carsi Vineyard Chardonnay or V. Sattui Dry Johannisburg Riesling.

**Robert O'Malley, Operations Manager
V. Sattui Winery**

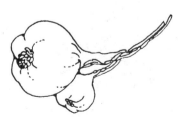

Angel-Hair Pasta Sauteed and Cooked in Fish Stock with Lobster

8 cups fish stock
2 live lobsters, 1 1/2 to 2 pounds each
3 tablespoons olive oil
4 large garlic cloves, chopped
1 1/2 pounds unpeeled tomatoes, pureed
1/2 teaspoon saffron (.2 grams) threads
1/2 teaspoon salt, or to taste

1/2 pound dried angel hair pasta, or coiled fedelini or capellini (very thin dried pasta noodles rolled into coils)

AS A GARNISH:
1 lemon, cut into 6 wedges
1/2 recipe Garlic Mayonnaise

In a narrow flameproof casserole or a stock pot, bring fish stock to a boil with 4 cups water. Drop in 1 lobster, it will turn pink. As soon as it stops moving, after a minute or two, remove lobster from pot and set it aside. Bring water back to a rapid boil before dropping in the next lobster. Reserve cooking water.

Separate lobster bodies from tails; grasp body in one hand and tail in the other, twist tail and pull; it will come free easily. Reserve any juices that ooze out. Pull out claws.

Bring lobster water to a boil again and add lobster bodies; simmer for 30 minutes, covered. Meanwhile, cut each tail, with its shell, crosswise into 3 pieces. Break claws (or remove meat from claws and discard shells, if preferred). Set aside.

Meanwhile, in a wide 2-quart saucepan, heat 1 tablespoon olive oil and add garlic. Cook until soft and add tomatoes; cook over medium-high heat for 3 minutes. Strain lobster water and juices into saucepan, bring to a boil, and reduce sauce to exactly 4 cups. Add saffron threads and salt; cover and set aside.

Heat remaining 2 tablespoons oil in a wide flameproof clay casserole or skillet. Add pasta, breaking it up with your hands in about 3-inch pieces as you add it. Over medium heat, stir pasta with a wooden spatula for 10 to 15 minutes, until it is golden brown (the more color the pasta acquires, the more flavor it will give to this dish; but be careful not to burn it).

Bring tomato sauce mixture to a boil and pour into casserole with noodles. Stir in lobster claws (or meat), together with tail sections. Cook over medium heat, stirring all the time, until the liquid is absorbed by the pasta. Cooking time will vary according to the size and material of casserole -- it will probably be 10 to 15 minutes. Taste for seasoning.

If you have used a clay casserole, surround pasta with lemon wedges, arrange lobster bodies on top, and serve directly from the casserole, passing the Garlic Mayonnaise * (alloili) in a sauce boat. Have guests squeeze a little lemon juice over their serving. Serves 6.

* In Catalunya, this dish is traditionally served with Garlic Mayonnaise on the side, although I find it really does not need it. MT

Wine Recommendation: Serve with an elegant oak-aged Chardonnay.

Marimar Torres

Marimar Torres, President of Torres Wines North America, and of the Torres Vineyard and Winery here in California, is also the author of two cookbooks, "The Spanish Table," and "The Catalan Country Kitchen." Her heritage in wines comes from her family who have been growers and vintners in Spain since the seventeenth century, Her keen interest in food developed in her first home in Catalunya, the rich, gastronomic region of northeastern Spain, and continues today in her new home in the California Wine Country.

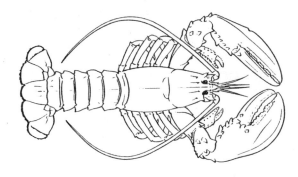

Grilled Scallop Salad with
Basil Vinaigrette Dressing

12 sea scallops

MARINADE:

1/2 cup olive oil	1 bunch of freshly chopped
1 teaspoon Dijon mustard	parsley
1 garlic clove, minced	Salt and pepper to taste

Combine marinade ingredients, add scallops and let stand for one hour at room temperature. Place two scallops on each skewer.

TO PREPARE SALAD:
2 bell peppers, preferably red and yellow
1 bunch arugula
Add mixture of mache and red oak leaf lettuce

Roast peppers, peel, seed and slice into julienne strips. Reserve separately. Clean lettuce greens. Combine and reserve.

BASIL VINAIGRETTE:

1/4 cup Balsamic vinegar	1-2 bunches basil, depending
1/4 cup sherry vinegar	upon desired flavor
1/2 orange, squeezed and juiced	1 1/2 cups extra virgin olive oil
2 shallots	Salt and pepper to taste
	1 anchovy filet, optional

In a blender or food processor, combine all ingredients except olive oil, until a smooth paste. With machine running, gradually add olive oil. Add salt and pepper. Set aside. Grill scallops for about 1 1/2 to 2 minutes.

Toss salad greens very lightly with basil vinaigrette dressing and divide onto glass serving plates. Top each plate with sliced scallops, julienned, roasted peppers and drizzle remaining dressing on top. Serve immediately. Serves 6.

Serve with Ferrari-Carano Alexander Valley Chardonnay.

Rhonda Carano, Co-Owner
Ferrari-Carano Vineyards and Winery

Seafood and Kielbasa Sausage Gumbo

1 pound kielbasa sausage
1 pound medium shrimp
3/4 pound fresh halibut filet (cut into 1/2-inch pieces)
3/4 pound fresh crabmeat
1 15-ounce can cut okra
1 cup Chardonnay
3/4 cup mixed vegetable oil and margarine
3/4 cup flour

2 cups chopped onions
2 cups chopped red or yellow bell peppers
1 1/2 cups chopped celery
1 tablespoon crushed garlic
6 cups seafood stock or clam juice
1 cup hot cooked rice, per serving

SEASONING MIX:

3 or 4 bay leaves
3/4 teaspoon salt
3/4 teaspoon cayenne pepper
1/2 teaspoon white pepper

1/4 teaspoon black pepper
1/4 teaspoon thyme
1/4 teaspoon oregano

Heat oil and margarine in large skillet over high heat until it smokes. Gradually whisk in flour and, whisking continuously, make a roux with dark brown consistency. Do not burn roux.

Immediately add 1/2 vegetables. Stir 2 minutes, add remaining vegetables. Add seasoning mix and garlic. Cook 3 to 4 minutes. In a 5-quart pot, add seafood stock and bring to a boil. Add roux mixture by spoonfuls, stirring until dissolved.

Add kielbasa sausage and continue boiling 15 minutes, stirring occasionally. Reduce heat and simmer 10 minutes more. Return to boil, add seafood, okra and wine. Remove from heat. Let stand 10 minutes to poach seafood. Skim any oil from surface. Serve immediately.

To serve, mound 1 cup cooked rice in middle of bowl and spoon a cup of gumbo over top.   Serves 8 to 10.

Serve with Eberle Chardonnay.

Eberle Winery

Linguini with Shrimp and Pesto

16-ounce package linguini, cooked to package directions

PESTO:

2-3 cloves fresh garlic
1/2 cup grated Parmesan cheese
2 cups fresh basil leaves

1/2 cup olive oil
1/2 cup low-fat sour cream

Puree ingredients for pesto in blender. Set aside.

SHRIMP MIXTURE:

1/2 pound sliced mushrooms (mix
 any varieties)
1 tablespoon olive oil
1/4 cup chopped green onions
Juice of one lemon
1/2 cup white wine

1 tablespoon Worcestershire
1 pound cleaned raw shrimp
1/2 cup chopped parsley
1 tomato, seeded and diced
4 ounces crumbled feta
 cheese

Saute sliced mushrooms in olive oil until tender. Add chopped green onions, lemon juice, wine and Worcestershire, then bring to a boil. Add shrimp and reduce heat to simmer, covered, until shrimp are done (uniformly pink in color).

Remove from heat and add pesto sauce to shrimp and stir until ingredients are thoroughly blended. Toss with hot linguini noodles, then add parsley, tomato and feta cheese. Toss lightly again before serving.   Serves 6.

Recommended wine: Lake Sonoma Winery 1990 Zinfandel.

Kate Moore
for
Lake Sonoma Winery

Crab Cakes with Baby Lettuce Salad and Ginger Dressing

CRAB CAKES:

1/2 pound fresh scallops
Salt and white pepper to taste
2 to 3 cups heavy cream
1 tablespoon chopped cilantro

3/4 pound fresh crab meat, shredded
1/2 cup diced tomatoes
1/4 cup chopped chives

Puree scallops, using on and off pulses until chopped fine. Then add cream and stir gently until it becomes a smooth thick paste. Don't overprocess. Season with salt and white pepper. Fold in the remaining ingredients. Cook the cakes in a medium hot saute pan with the barest amount of oil. Cook these just before serving.

GINGER DRESSING:

3 tablespoons fresh ginger, finely chopped
1 teaspoon fresh chives, chopped
1 teaspoon fresh cilantro, finely chopped

1/2 cup dry white wine
1/4 cup rice wine vinegar
1 cup light canola oil
Salt and pepper to taste

Puree in a blender. Make salad of baby lettuce. Toss the lettuce with the dressing. Serve the salad and crab cake side by side on a 10-inch plate. Serves 6.

Serve with Mumm Cuvée Napa Valley Brut Prestige.

**Elaine Bell, Culinary Director
for
Mumm Cuvée Napa**

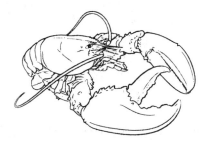

Easy Dill and Garlic Shrimp

1/2 pound medium raw shrimp,
 peeled and cleaned
1 teaspoon dill weed
2 cloves garlic, minced
1/2 cup light sour cream
1 tablespoon butter or margarine
1 tablespoon flour

3/4 cup milk
1/2 cup white wine
1/4 cup chopped parsley
Freshly grated Parmesan
 cheese
Freshly ground black pepper
16-ounce package dry fettucini

Prepare fettucini according to package directions, and prepare sauce while pasta is cooking.

Melt butter or margarine in large skillet, and lightly saute garlic just enough to release flavor. Add flour and blend thoroughly, then add milk, stirring constantly over low heat to make white sauce. Add wine, blending into sauce.

Add shrimp and dill and simmer, covered, until shrimp is uniformly pink in color. Fold in sour cream and mix with hot fettucini. Top with parsley, Parmesan cheese and freshly ground black pepper.

Serves 6.

Recommended wine: Lake Sonoma Winery 1989 Sauvignon Blanc.

Kate Moore
for
Lake Sonoma Winery

Poultry

SPICES OF THE WORLD

Mushroom Gloss Chicken Breasts

2 medium-large frying chicken
  breasts, split, boned and skinned
Salt and freshly ground white
  pepper
3 tablespoons unsalted butter
1 cup lean chicken broth
1/2 cup heavy (whipping) cream

Cognac mushrooms (recipe
  below)
1 tablespoon Cognac or
  Brandy
1 egg yolk
2 tablespoons finely chopped
  curly parsley

Pat breast pieces between sheets of waxed paper to an even 5/8-inch thickness. Season with salt and pepper. Heat butter in a large heavy frying pan over medium heat until it bubbles. Add breasts and cook, occasionally turning until opaque almost to center, about 5 minutes total. Remove to slightly warm serving plates. Spoon mushrooms over breasts. Remove any excess butter from chicken pan, leaving brown (not burned) drippings. Add broth and cream to pan and cook over high heat, stirring, until reduced to 1 cup liquid. Remove from heat. Whisk Cognac with yolks; whisk in a little of the cream sauce. Gradually whisk yolk mixture into cream sauce. Heat and stir over low heat just until sauce thickens slightly (do not allow to bubble). Stir in parsley. Season with salt and pepper. Pour over breasts. Accompany with peeled little new potatoes which have been cooked, then heated and turned in butter to give a golden finish. Sprinkle with parsley.

Serves 4.

COGNAC MUSHROOMS:

3/4 pound thinly sliced mushrooms
4 tablespoons unsalted butter

1/4 cup Cognac or Brandy
Salt to taste

Heat 4 tablespoons unsalted butter in a large heavy frying pan over medium-high heat. Add 3/4 pound very thinly sliced mushrooms. Cook and turn occasionally until liquid disappears and mushrooms are edged with a toastiness. Add 1/4 cup Cognac or Brandy and continue cooking until Cognac disappears and mushrooms again have an edge of toastiness. Season with salt.

Serve with Mumm Cuvée Napa Valley Brut Prestige.

Shirley Sarvis
Consultant and Food Writer
for
Mumm Cuvée Napa

Mar Y Montana
Chicken with Prawns

1 pound prawns (20-25 to pound)
6 chicken breasts, boneless and
 skinless
1 tablespoon butter
Salt and freshly ground black
 pepper to taste

1/4 cup flour
1 teaspoon salt
1/2 teaspoon pepper
1/2 teaspoon cinnamon
1 bay leaf
1 tablespoon olive oil

Peel the prawns and set aside. Put the shells in a small sauce pan with the bay leaf and cover with 5 cups of water. Bring to a boil, reduce heat and cook for 15 minutes. Drain, reserving the stock. Discard the shells.

Put the flour, salt, pepper and cinnamon in a bowl. Dip the chicken breasts into the flour mixture, coating the breasts on both sides. Heat the butter and 1 tablespoon olive oil in a skillet. Cook the chicken until golden on both sides. Remove the chicken. In the same skillet, cook the prawns half a minute on each side. Remove the prawns. In a large skillet or preferably a clay casserole that can go to the table, heat the Sofrito and stir in the Picada. This creates the sauce.

PICADA:

1 ounce unsweetened chocolate,
 minced or grated
3 cloves garlic, peeled and
 chopped
1/4 cup whole toasted almonds

1 tablespoon parsley
Pinch of fresh thyme and
 fresh oregano

In a mortar, grind together the chocolate, garlic, toasted almonds, parsley, thyme and oregano. Add a little of the reduced stock and grind the mixture to a paste. Set aside.

SOFRITO:

2 tablespoons olive oil
1 onion, minced
3/4 pound tomatoes, peeled,
 seeded and chopped

2 tablespoons Anise Brandy
1 cup dry white wine

Heat 2 tablespoons of olive oil in a non-reactive skillet. Cook the onions until golden. Add the tomatoes and cook until dry. Stir in the Brandy, wine and reserved stock. Cook until reduced by half.

Add chicken to the sauce and cook for 5 minutes. Stir in the prawns. Taste for salt and pepper and add if necessary. Cook for another 5 minutes, or until the chicken and prawns are cooked through and the sauce is thickened. Serve directly from the casserole.   Serves 6.

Serve with Gloria Ferrer Sonoma County Brut.

Ann Walker
for
Gloria Ferrer Champagne Caves

This recipe by Ann Walker, Chef, Lecturer and Writer, is also in her book, "A Season in Spain."

Martini Roast Chicken

1 Roasting chicken or capon
Olive Oil

STUFFING:

2 cups cooked chard - veins
 removed
1/2 cup thinly sliced green onion
1/2 cup pine nuts
1 cup bread crumbs

1/4 cup grated Parmesan
 cheese
1/4 teaspoon nutmeg
1 teaspoon poultry seasoning
1/2 teaspoon salt
1 egg

On a low heat in 1/4-inch of olive oil, saute onions until transparent and sweet tasting. Add pine nuts and cook a minute or two. Drain chard and chop fairly fine. Add to onions. Add the rest of the ingredients.

Wash inside of chicken. Make a rinse of wine and water, and rinse out. Stuff the cavity, saving a little bit for the neck opening. Place a crust of bread at the opening of the body cavity to hold stuffing in. Pull skin as close together as possible. Put skewers across and lace together, using the end of the string to tie legs in. Stuff the neck cavity and bring skin flap back and fasten. Roast on a rack at 325 degrees for 1 1/2 to 2 hours.

Serve with Louis M. Martini Gewurztraminer.

Louis M. Martini Winery

Mendocino Quail Salad with Orange-Mint Dressing

4 quail or 2 Cornish game hens, split and backbone flattened
1/2 pound mixed greens

1 medium orange, peeled and sectioned
Mint sprigs
10 cherry tomatoes, halved

MARINADE:

1/4 cup white wine vinegar
2 tablespoons olive oil
1/4 cup Chardonnay
1/4 cup fresh orange juice
1/4 cup chopped onion

4 tablespoons chopped fresh mint
1/2 teaspoon crushed white peppercorns
Pinch of salt

Combine and mix marinade thoroughly. Cover quail with marinade and refrigerate for at least 2 hours.

VINAIGRETTE:

4 tablespoons chopped fresh mint
1 tablespoon chopped shallots
2 tablespoons white wine vinegar
6 tablespoons fresh orange juice
1 teaspoon honey

1/4 cup plain low-fat yogurt
1 tablespoon walnut oil
Salt, pepper and pinch of ground cloves to taste

Combine and mix vinaigrette thoroughly. Refrigerate.

Remove quail and pat dry.

Grill quail, skin side down, for 4 to 5 minutes over hot coals, turn and continue cooking for 2 to 3 more minutes; or place under broiler for 3 to 4 minutes per side. (Cornish game hens require approximately 8 to 10 minutes grilling or broiling per side.)

Divide greens evenly on plates. Garnish with orange sections, mint sprigs, and tomato. Top with quail (or halved game hen) and dressing. Recommended wine: Fetzer Sundial Chardonnay.

Serve 2 as an entree.

**Chef John Ash, Culinary Director
Fetzer Vineyards**

Grilled Chicken Breast
with Blackbean and Roasted Corn Salsa

8 boneless, skinless chicken breast
halves
1 1/2 cups dried blackbeans (soak
overnight in water)
2 garlic cloves, chopped
4 ears of corn
1/2 cup red bell peppers, finely
chopped
1/4 cup red onion, finely chopped
1 1/2 tablespoons red vinegar
1/2 tablespoon Balsamic vinegar

1/2 tablespoon fresh lime juice
1/2 teaspoon ground
coriander
1 teaspoon oregano
1/4 cup Italian parsley,
chopped
1/4 cup cilantro, chopped
6 ounces olive oil
Salt and freshly ground
pepper to taste

Marinate the chicken breasts in 4 ounces of the olive oil and the stems of the fresh herbs (which may be chopped slightly) for eight hours.

Remove husks from the corn, and lightly coat with a little of the olive oil. Place on a baking sheet and roast at 350 degrees for about 40 minutes or until kernels are golden brown. Cool at room temperature, then remove kernels, scraping the cobbs and saving any liquid along with the kernels.

Drain the beans and put into a saucepan with 1 teaspoon salt, cover with water and cook over medium heat until tender. Drain.

Sweat the garlic and red onions in the remaining olive oil, add the peppers and coriander, and cook for 2 more minutes. Stir in the beans and corn, then add vinegars and lime juice. Heat to a simmer (if more liquid is needed to moisten the salsa, use chicken stock or water). Simmer for 5 minutes. Remove from heat and mix in the parsley, cilantro and oregano. Season with salt and freshly ground pepper.

Simply take the chicken from the marinade, season with salt and freshly ground pepper. Grill both sides until done, about 3 to 4 minutes depending on the size of the breasts.

Serve salsa under the grilled chicken breasts and garnish with cilantro sprigs. Serves 8.

Serve with Chateau Souverain Sauvignon Blanc.

Martin W. Courtman, Executive Chef
Chateau Souverain

Tarragon Chicken Breast Chardonnay

4 chicken breast halves, boned
 and skinned
8 ounces fresh sliced mushrooms
1/2 cup green onions, sliced
2 tablespoons shallots, minced
1 ounce oil-packed sundried
 tomatoes, minced

2 tablespoons olive oil
1/2 cup clear chicken broth
1/2 cup Chardonnay
1/2 cup heavy cream
2 tablespoons flour
Salt and pepper to taste
1 teaspoon dried tarragon

Mix flour, salt and pepper in shallow dish and lightly coat chicken breasts, reserving balance of flour. Place oil in saute skillet and heat to medium temperature. Brown chicken on all sides and saute approximately 10 minutes. Add mushrooms, onions, shallots, tomatoes and tarragon, and cook 2 minutes longer. Add Chardonnay and chicken broth, reserving 2 tablespoons and heat. Then add remaining flour, mixed with 2 tablespoons reserved chicken broth. Stir until smooth. Add cream, lower heat and simmer to desired consistency.
Serves 4.

Serve with lightly chilled Round Hill Chardonnay.

Charles Abela, President
Round Hill Vineyards

Mushroom-Pepper Chicken

2 1/2 pounds chicken, cut into
 serving pieces
3/4 cup white wine
8 sliced fresh mushrooms
1 medium onion, minced
1 tablespoon paprika
1 clove garlic, minced
1 teaspoon marjoram leaves,
 crushed

1/4 teaspoon salt
1/8 teaspoon ground black
 pepper
1 teaspoon cornstarch
2/3 cup plain low-fat yogurt (at
 room temperature
1 tablespoon parsley,
 chopped fine

Remove skin from chicken pieces. In a large heavy skillet, brown
chicken on all sides, adding a few drops of water to start chicken
browning. Add mushrooms, minced onion, paprika, minced garlic,
marjoram, salt, black pepper and wine. Simmer covered until chicken
juices run clear when pierced with a sharp knife, about 35 minutes.
Blend cornstarch with 2 tablespoons water; stir into skillet. Cook and
stir until thickened, about 2 minutes. Stir yogurt with a fork until
smooth. Stir into liquid in skillet. Cook over low heat until hot. Serve
sprinkled with parsley.   Serves 4.

Serve with J. Wile & Sons Sauvignon Blanc.

Bergfeld Winery

Chicken Scallops with Tomato, Oakleaf Lettuce and Fresh Basil

2 whole chicken breasts, split, skinned and boned
2 eggs
1 cup bread crumbs
1 tablespoon minced fresh rosemary
1 tablespoon minced fresh sage
1 tablespoon minced fresh parsley
Salt and pepper to taste
Olive oil for frying

6 ripe fresh tomatoes, cut into small chunks
1 1/2 cups oakleaf lettuce
1 tablespoon coarsely chopped fresh basil
2 tablespoons extra virgin olive oil
A splash of Balsamic vinegar
Lemon wedges

Gently pound chicken breasts to flatten them. Lightly beat eggs in bowl. On a plate, combine bread crumbs with sage, rosemary and parsley, season with fresh ground pepper. Dip chicken breasts into egg wash, then coat both sides with bread crumb mixture. Shake off excess. Meanwhile, heat frying pan, adding your olive oil to saute each chicken breast, about 4 to 5 minutes on each side. Salt chicken breasts, once each side has been fried. Transfer to paper towels and let drain.

Combine tomatoes, oakleaf lettuce and coarsely chopped basil with extra virgin olive oil and a splash of vinegar. Season with salt and pepper.

Arrange the chicken breasts on a platter and spoon salad mixture on side.   Serves 4.

Serve with Ferrari-Carano Alexander Valley Chardonnay.

Rhonda Carano, Co-Owner
Ferrari-Carano Vineyards and Winery

Chicken Curry

1 medium-size chicken, 3 1/2 to 4
 pounds
1 teaspoon chili powder
2 teaspoons curry powder
1/2 teaspoon saffron powder
Salt to taste
2 medium red peppers
2 cloves garlic

1 large onion, chopped
1 tablespoon vinegar
1 cup milk
1 1/2 cups chicken broth
1 stick cinnamon
1 piece ginger, about 1 1/2
 inches

Cut chicken into serving pieces and put in large pan. Cut onion and red peppers in small pieces. Crush garlic. Add all this to chicken in pan. Mix chicken broth with curry powder, chili powder, saffron, salt and vinegar. Add to chicken with the rest of ingredients, except the milk. Simmer until half done. Then add the milk. Continue simmering. When done, remove chicken to plate and strain broth. Remove skin and bones from chicken and break or cut into large pieces. Thicken the broth with flour. Return the chicken to broth.

Serve with white rice and small bowls of crisp chopped bacon, chopped hard boiled eggs, coconut, chopped peanuts and chutney.
Serves 4 to 6.

Serve with Freemark Abbey Johannisberg Riesling.

Freemark Abbey Vineyard

Ginger

Roasted Cornish Game Hens

6 Cornish game hens

STUFFING (FOR 6 HENS):

1 cup long grain white rice	1/4 teaspoon ground
2 cups chicken stock	cardamom
1/2 teaspoon salt	1 teaspoon orange rind,
1 tablespoon butter	freshly grated
1/4 teaspoon ground cinnamon	1/2 cup chopped pitted dates
	1/2 cup chopped pecans

Bring chicken stock, salt, butter, cinnamon, cardamom and orange rind to a boil. Add rice, cover and reduce heat. Simmer 20 minutes and let sit 5 minutes. Fluff with fork and stir in dates and pecans.

Preheat oven to 350 degrees.

Prepare the birds as follows:

6 Cornish game hens	1/2 cup orange marmalade
Salt and pepper	1/4 cup Gewurztraminer
6 tablespoons butter, softened	

Rinse game hens and pat dry. Salt and pepper cavity, and stuff with a generous 1/2 cup of rice mixture. Secure legs with kitchen string and place hens in a roasting pan. Brush hens with softened butter and roast for 30 minutes.

Melt orange marmalade with the wine and reduce slightly. Raise oven temperature to 400 degrees. Baste hens with marmalade mixture and continue roasting an additional 20 or 30 minutes, or until juices run clear and hens are browned. Baste occasionally with the marmalade mixture, and if the hens start to darken too much, cover with aluminum foil.   Serves 6.

Serve with Louis M. Martini Gewurztraminer.

Louis M. Martini Winery

Roast Squab with Fennel in Four Fashions

2 celery roots, trimmed and
quartered (cook with potatoes)
4 full squab (double) breasts,
boneless
1 russet potato; peeled, quartered
and cooked in salted water
1 tablespoon cream

2 tablespoons butter
5 fennel bulbs, trim off frawns
and stem
2 cups squab stock
1 cup Pinot Noir
1 tablespoon fennel seeds

TO ROAST FENNEL:

Toss fennel bulbs lightly in olive oil, salt and pepper. Wrap each in aluminum foil and place on a sheet pan. Roast at 450 degrees for 1 hour or until soft. Let cool, then unwrap. Take two of the bulbs and remove any dark spots, blend in a blender or food processor. Boil the celery roots and potato and put through a ricer to make mashed potatoes. Add butter and a pinch of salt. Fold the strained fennel puree into the mashed celery/potato mixture and add the cream. The potato-fennel puree should be thick enough to stand up.

Take the other two fennel bulbs and cut into slender wedges. Place on a sheet pan, drizzle with olive oil, sprinkle with salt and pepper. Turn on broiler.

Season and brown the squab breasts, remove, drain fat from the pan and add pinot noir and fennel seeds. Reduce to light syrup. Add squab stock and reduce to 1/2 cup. Adjust sauce with butter and salt.

With the last raw fennel bulb, shave across the grain as thinly as possible. Toss lightly in flour and deep fry until just golden on the edges. Remove to paper towel and salt.

FOR PRESENTATION:

Roast squab to medium rare, broil roasted fennel wedges until light brown. Place 5 ounces of fennel puree in center of plate. Lean two wedges of fennel on either side and, in between, place squab breast. Surround with fennel jus and top with fried fennel shavings. Serves 4.

Wine Suggestion: Meridian Pinot Noir or Napa Ridge Pinot Noir

Jerry Comfort, Executive Chef
Beringer Vineyards

Tandoori-Style Roast Chicken

1 teaspoon salt
Juice of 1 lemon
2 minced garlic cloves
2 tablespoons minced fresh ginger
1 teaspoon ground cumin seeds
1 teaspoon ground cardamom
 seeds
2 teaspoons curry powder

1 teaspoon paprika
1/2 cup plain yogurt
1 4-pound roasting chicken
1 teaspoon black pepper
2 teaspoons salt
1 tablespoon olive oil
1/2 cup lemon juice

Mix together in a small bowl the first nine ingredients. Set aside. Preheat oven to 400 degrees.

Remove giblets from chicken and scatter over the bottom of a roasting pan. Rinse chicken thoroughly inside and out, and pat dry. Mix pepper and salt and rub into the walls of the interior cavity. Run your fingers under the skin of the breast and legs, separating it gently from the meat underneath.

Distribute as evenly as possible the herb mixture between the skin and meat, then rub the olive oil over the skin of the chicken.

Place the chicken, breast-side down, on top of the giblets and roast for 30 minutes, basting after 15 minutes with the lemon juice.

Reduce heat to 375 degrees, turn the chicken breast-side up, baste once more, then roast 15 minutes longer, or until the skin is a golden brown and a thermometer inserted into the thickest part of the thigh registers between 170 and 175 degrees.

Let rest 10 minutes before carving.   Serves 2 to 4.

Serve with Sattui Suzanne's Vineyard Zinfandel.

**Robert O'Malley, Operations Manager
V. Sattui Winery**

Breast of Squab with Chipotle Molé, Rattlesnake Beans and Leek Tumbleweed

4 squab
Fresh ground cumin
Salt and pepper
1 cup rich squab stock, reduced to light demi-glace
1 cup Syrah, reduced to 2 tablespoons
1/2 Chipotle chili, soaked, de-seeded and pureed

1/2 ancho chili, soaked, de-seeded and pureed
2 teaspoons bitter chocolate
2 tablespoons cilantro
1/2 cup raspberries
2 leeks for crispy fried leek rings
8 ounces dried rattlesnake or pinto beans

TO PREPARE THE BEANS:

Soak rattlesnake or pinto beans overnight, then thoroughly cook in chicken stock. Reheat the beans in the stock. Then, before service, drain and add to molé.

TO PREPARE SQUAB:

Season the squab with cumin, salt and pepper. Brown in a hot saute pan in a little olive oil. Roast at 400 degrees approximately 15 minutes or until medium rare. Let squab rest, then remove breast and legs. Reserve the carcass for the squab stock.

SQUAB STOCK:

Prepare 1 quart chicken stock using lightly roasted bones. Reserve all bones from the squab. Saute 1/2 of an onion and 1/2 carrot in butter until golden. Add the bones and 1/3 of the chicken stock. Simmer until reduced to 1/2 cup. Add another 1/3 of the chicken stock, and again, simmer until reduced to 3/4 cup. Add final 1/3 of the chicken stock and reduce to a total of 1 cup stock. Strain. Separately, reduce 1 cup Syrah to a syrup. Add to the strained squab demi-glace.

TO MAKE THE MOLÉ SAUCE:

Season the squab demi with 1 teaspoon chipotle chili puree, 2 teaspoons ancho chile puree and 2 teaspoons bitter chocolate. Add warmed beans to molé sauce and, just before serving, add raspberries and cilantro.

TO MAKE CRISPY FRIED LEEKS:

Cut the white and light green off the leek as thinly as possible into rings. Separate rings, wash and dry. In small batches, dust the leeks with flour and deep fry at 325 degrees until the first signs of brown appear. Remove and drain. Salt, then reheat to order.

FINAL PRESENTATION:

Mound beans in center of plate, letting sauce run out from underneath. Top with squab and fried leek tumbleweed.

Wine Suggestions: Meridian Syrah or Chateau Souverain Zinfandel

Jerry Comfort, Executive Chef
Beringer Vineyards

Happy Duck

2 5-pound ducks
6 ounces plum jam
1 cup Pinot Noir or Late Harvest
wine
1/2 cup rice wine vinegar
1/4 cup soy sauce

1 2-inch square of ginger
4 tablespoons basil, chopped
4 cloves garlic, peeled
1/2 onion, chopped
1 jalapeno pepper, seeded

Prick duck all over with a fork. Place it in a steamer with an inch of water. Simmer for 50 to 60 minutes. Remove and cool duck. (This can be done the day before the barbecue.)

Cut duck into serving-size pieces.

In a food processor, combine all the rest of the ingredients and puree. Marinate the duck pieces in puree for 1 hour.

Barbecue duck by placing a drip pan in the center of the barbecue and place hot coals around it. Place the duck in the center over the drip pan and put the lid on the barbecue. Cook until the skin is brown and duck is done to taste.

This dish is a wonderful accompaniment to Robert Stemmler Pinot Noir.

Robert Stemmler
Robert Stemmler Vineyards

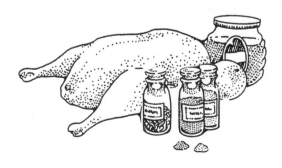

Vegetables

SPICES OF THE WORLD

Onions in White Burgundy Cream

2 pounds small white onions
1 1/2 cups White Burgundy or
Chardonnay
6 tablespoons butter
1 bay leaf
1/2 teaspoon dried thyme,
crumbled

1/2 teaspoon salt
1/4 teaspoon white pepper
1 teaspoon grated lemon rind
2 tablespoons flour
1/2 cup heavy cream
2 tablespoons chopped
parsley

Blanch onions in boiling water for 1 minute. Drain, rinse under cold running water, and peel. In skillet, combine wine, 4 tablespoons butter, bay leaf, thyme, salt, pepper and lemon rind. Bring to a boil. Add onions. Cover and simmer about 20 minutes, turning onions occasionally, until tender. Remove onions with slotted spoon. Boil cooking liquid until reduced to about 1 cup. Strain, if desired. In medium saucepan, combine flour with 2 tablespoons butter and cook for 1 minute. Slowly whisk in reduced liquid and cream. Bring to a boil over medium heat, stirring constantly. Add onions, lower heat and continue cooking just until onions are heated through. Transfer to heated serving bowls. Sprinkle with chopped parsley.   Serves 8.

Serve with Mirassou Chardonnay.

Mirassou

Spicy Broccoli

3 cups broccoli florets
1 medium onion, chopped
1/4 cup fresh parsley, chopped
1/4 cup white wine
1 teaspoon grated lemon peel
(fresh)

2 teaspoons basil
1/4 teaspoon dried crushed
 red pepper
2 tablespoons olive oil
1/2 cup grated Parmesan
 cheese

Steam broccoli until just tender, 3 to 4 minutes.

Heat olive oil in medium frying pan over medium heat. Add chopped onion and saute until soft, about 6 minutes. Add chopped parsley, lemon peel, wine , basil and crushed red pepper. Stir while cooking, 2 minutes. Add broccoli and toss until coated. Add salt and pepper to taste. Sprinkle cheese on top. Serves 4.

Bergfeld Winery

Ragout of Vegetables

1 cup zucchini, cut batonette
1 cup red bell peppers, cut
batonette
1 cup yellow bell peppers, cut
batonette
2 cups mushrooms, sliced

1 cup white onions, sliced
2 tablespoons fresh tarragon,
 chopped
2 cloves garlic, minced
1 cup sweet butter
Salt and pepper

Heat the butter in a large Dutch oven until very hot. Add the onions and cook until translucent. Stir in the red and yellow peppers and allow to cook 2 to 3 minutes. Add the mushrooms, garlic and tarragon. Simmer for 15 minutes. Season with salt and pepper. Serves 4 to 6.

Elaine Bell, Culinary Director
Sterling Vineyards

Onion-Parsley Potato Bake

2 large onions, chopped
4 medium potatoes, cut in pieces
1 cup water
1 cup milk
Salt and pepper to taste
2 tablespoons butter

2 tablespoons fresh chopped
 parsley
1/4 cup grated Parmesan
 cheese
1 tablespoon additional butter

Simmer potatoes, onions, milk and water in covered pan until tender.

Drain, reserving liquid. Mash potatoes with butter, salt and pepper. Add reserved liquid as needed to mash. If there is not enough liquid, use additional milk. Mix in parsley. Place potatoes in a buttered casserole. Sprinkle cheese on top. Dot with butter. Bake for 20 minutes, or until topping has browned. Serves 4 to 6.

Sutter Home Winery

Spiced Carrots

2 cups carrots, cut in thin strips
3/4 cup pineapple juice
3/4 teaspoon ground cinnamon

1/8 teaspoon ground nutmeg
Sprinkling of black pepper

In a saucepan, combine carrots, pineapple juice, cinnamon, nutmeg and pepper. Bring to a boil. Reduce heat to simmer. Cook, covered, about 15 minutes until carrots are crisp-tender. Serves 4 to 6.

Freemark Abbey Vineyard

Potato and Butternut Squash Gratin with Caramelized Onions and Fresh Thyme

4 large white skinned potatoes
1 small butternut squash, peeled and seeded
4 large onions, peeled and cut into 1/2-inch slices
1/2 cup plus 2 tablespoons unsalted butter
4 cloves garlic, finely minced or pressed

2 tablespoons chopped fresh thyme
Salt and freshly ground pepper to taste
3/4 cup toasted bread crumbs, seasoned with olive oil, garlic and salt and pepper to taste
3 tablespoons extra virgin olive oil

Butter a 9 by 13-inch baking dish with the 2 tablespoons butter. Sprinkle one clove of the pressed garlic over the bottom of the pan and set it aside.

Caramelize the onions by sauteing the onions in the remaining butter over medium heat until all are translucent. Continue to stir the onions as they begin to brown. The onions are done when they have reached a true caramel color -- they should be quite brown for the best flavor. They do take a long time! Set aside.

While the onions are caramelizing, slice both the potatoes and the butternut squash into very thin slices. Begin to assemble the gratin. In the prepared baking dish arrange a layer of half the potatoes in bottom of dish. Sprinkle with a little salt and pepper. Using half of the sliced butternut squash, arrange a layer on top of the potatoes. Sprinkle second clove of pressed garlic over the squash and again sprinkle with salt and pepper. Sprinkle one tablespoon of the thyme over this layer.

Now evenly spread the caramelized onions over the squash layer. Repeat the layering process with remaining squash, another clove of the garlic, the salt and pepper, and the remaining thyme. Layer the remaining potatoes over the squash, sprinkle with the garlic and the salt and pepper. Drizzle the olive oil over the top of the gratin.

Cover the gratin with foil and bake at 375 degrees for one hour or until potatoes and squash are done. Remove foil, sprinkle seasoned bread crumbs on top of the gratin and bake another 6 to 7 minutes. Remove from oven, cut into squares, and serve while hot.

Makes 10 to 12 side dish servings.

Kristine A. Schug
Schug Carneros Estate Winery

Kristine Schug, formerly of Trilogy Restaurant in the Napa Valley, has recently joined her husband, Axel, at the family owned and operated Schug Carneros Estate Winery. Now Hospitality Director as well as in-house chef, Kristine has brought her culinary experience with her, as well as her knowledge of food and wine pairing from her past experience at Domain Carneros and Beringer Vineyards.

Mediterranean Green Beans

1 pound fresh green beans, cut
into 1 1/2-inch pieces
1 cup chopped tomatoes
1 medium onion, sliced thin
1/2 garlic clove, minced
1 teaspoon thyme leaves

1 teaspoon paprika
1/16 teaspoon black pepper
1 strip orange rind
1 tablespoon olive oil
1 cup water

In medium saucepan, heat oil, add onion and saute until golden, about 1 minute. Add tomatoes, garlic, paprika, thyme, black pepper, orange strip and 1 cup water. Bring to boil, reduce heat and simmer 5 minutes before adding beans. Cook, covered, until crisp tender, about 10 minutes. Remove orange rind before serving. Serves 4.

Sutter Home Winery

Tomato-Zucchini Bake

3 cups zucchini, sliced thin
4 fresh tomatoes, sliced
1/4 cup fresh white bread crumbs
2 tablespoons fresh chopped
parsley
1/2 clove garlic, minced fine

1 medium onion, sliced thin
1 1/2 teaspoons chili powder
Salt and pepper to taste
1 tablespoon olive oil
2 tablespoons Parmesan
cheese, grated

Preheat oven to 375 degrees. In a lightly greased 6-cup casserole, layer half the zucchini, tomatoes and onion. Sprinkle with half of the parsley and seasonings. Repeat layering with balance of zucchini, tomatoes and onion. Season again. Top with bread crumbs that have been mixed with olive oil. Sprinkle grated cheese on top.

Bake, uncovered, until vegetables are tender, about 35 to 40 minutes.
Serves 4.

Kunde Estate Winery

Baked Sweet Potatoes with Apples

2-quart baking dish, well buttered	1/2 teaspoon ground
4 large sweet potatoes (3-4	cinnamon
pounds)	1/2 teaspoon salt
2 large tart apples, peeled and	1/8 teaspoon white pepper
sliced	4 tablespoons butter
1/2 cup Riesling and Chenin Blanc	

Boil potatoes for 25 minutes. Cool, peel and cut into 1/8-inch slices. Layer potatoes and apple slices in casserole, beginning and ending with potatoes. Combine wine and seasonings. Add to casserole. Dot top with butter. Cover tightly and bake at 350 degrees for 20 minutes. Remove cover and continue baking for another 20 minutes.

Serves 4 to 6.

Mirassou

Roasted Red Potatoes with Garlic and Thyme

8-10 small red potatoes
10 cloves of garlic
1 tablespoon thyme if dried, double if fresh
1/4 cup olive oil

Wash the potatoes and pat dry with a paper towel. Cut them in half and place in a glass baking dish. Peel the garlic cloves, leaving them whole, and sprinkle them among the potatoes in the pan. Pour the olive oil over the potatoes and garlic, then sprinkle with the thyme. Bake in a 375 degree oven for about an hour, or until the potatoes are soft when poked with a fork. Season with salt and pepper to taste.

Serves 4.

An easy, flavorful way to roast potatoes.

Windsor Vineyards

Roasted Garlic Cloves

2 cups peeled garlic cloves
1/2 to 3/4 cup olive oil
Salt
Pepper - freshly ground to taste
2 tablespoons rosemary, fresh if
 possible

1 tablespoon thyme (fresh is
 best, but dried is fine, too)
1/4 teaspoon chili pepper
 flakes

In a glass, oven-proof baking dish (12 X 14 inches) scatter garlic cloves, salt and pepper, rosemary, thyme and chili pepper flakes. Drizzle olive oil over all. Cover pan with aluminum foil. Bake in 350 degree oven for 1 hour or until cloves are nicely browned and glazed.

Use several ways: As is, spread on bread, or pureed to use in place of butter makes a nice addition to soups and dressings. This keeps very well refrigerated.

The nutty quality of the garlic is great with Christopher Creek 1990 Syrah.

Susan Mitchell, President and Co-Owner
Christopher Creek Winery

Sauces
and
Condiments

SPICES OF THE WORLD

Mushroom Cream Sauce with Tarragon

Serve with unseasoned chicken breasts grilled, sauteed or broiled

4 ounces (1 stick) unsalted butter
1 pound button mushrooms, thinly sliced
1 cup chicken stock (unsalted or low-salt, preferably homemade)
2/3 cup heavy cream
2 tablespoons parsley, finely chopped

2 tablespoons fresh tarragon, finely chopped or 1 teaspoon dried

GARNISH:
1 tablespoons unsalted butter
1/3 cup pine nuts (pignoli)

In butter, saute mushrooms over medium heat, stirring frequently until tender. Add chicken stock and continue cooking, stirring occasionally, until liquid is reduce by half. Add cream; continue cooking and stirring until liquid is again reduced by half. Add parsley and tarragon and cook briefly, stirring to blend flavors. For garnish, saute pine nuts in butter over medium heat until golden brown on both sides. Sprinkle over sauce.   Makes 2 cups, serves 8.

This recipe was developed for Kendall-Jackson's Proprietor's Grand Reserve Chardonnay. This full-bodied wine has rich flavors of vanilla, butter and butterscotch, along with lemon and tropical pineapple fruit. Round and smooth on the palate, the wine can stand up to a full-flavored, butter cream sauce. Its slight hint of licorice ties in nicely with licorice-like herbs, such as tarragon or chervil.

Kendall-Jackson Vineyard

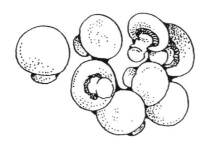

Mediterranean Medley

Serve with unseasoned chicken breasts, grilled, sauteed or broiled.

3 tablespoons olive oil
1/2 cup onions, finely chopped
3 cloves garlic, very finely chopped
2 green onions, thinly sliced (white part plus 2 inches of green)
2 medium carrots, very finely chopped
2 medium zucchini, very finely chopped (peels on)

1/2 tablespoon lemon juice
1/2 teaspoon lemon zest
3 sundried tomatoes (oil packed) very finely chopped
2 tablespoons fresh basil, very finely chopped or 1 teaspoon dried

In olive oil, saute onions and garlic over low heat until they begin to soften. Add green onions, carrots and zucchini; cook slowly until tender. Stir in lemon juice, lemon zest and sundried tomatoes. Cook briefly, stirring to blend flavors. Add basil at last minute. Add salt if necessary.   Makes 2 cups, serves 8.

This recipe was developed for Kendall-Jackson Vintner's Reserve Sauvignon Blanc. This light-to-medium bodied wine has the classic Sauvignon balance of citrus fruit with hints of herbs and green grass. Brief aging in oak rounds it out and adds a touch of vanilla. Its crisp acidity suits it to slightly tart dishes, and its herbal flavors make it a natural for Mediterranean herbs and vegetables.

Kendall-Jackson Vineyard

Wild Mushroom Sauce
with Rosemary and Bacon

Serve with unseasoned beef, grilled, sauteed or broiled.

1/4 cup olive oil
1/2 cup bacon, finely chopped
1 medium red bell pepper, finely
 chopped
6 medium cloves garlic, finely
 chopped
1/4 teaspoon fresh or dried
 rosemary, very finely chopped

2 cups fresh shiitake
 (Chinese-style black)
 mushrooms, finely chopped
 (6 large mushrooms, stems
 removed). Can use regular
 mushrooms, but flavor will be
 less intense.
1/4 cup unsalted or low-salt
 beef broth, preferably
 homemade

In olive oil, saute bacon over low heat until it begins to soften. Add
red bell pepper and garlic, saute slowly, stirring frequently, until well
coated with oil and slightly softened. Add mushrooms; mix well and
cover pan. Cook over low heat, stirring occasionally, until mushrooms
have released their liquid. Uncover pan, add rosemary and broth, and
continue cooking until liquid is almost all evaporated. Add salt if
necessary.   Makes 2 cups, serves 8.

*This recipe was developed for Kendall-Jackson's Vintner's Reserve
Cabernet Sauvignon. This wine has a medium body, with flavors of
cherries and spicy pepper and cinnamon. Oak aging adds a toasty
quality and smooths out the tannins. It stands up nicely to the meaty
black mushrooms and its mildly herbal flavors match well with the red
bell pepper and rosemary.*

Kendall-Jackson Vineyard

Rosemary

Cajun Spice Butter

1 pound sweet butter, room
temperature
1 teaspoon cayenne
4 teaspoons paprika
4 teaspoons garlic powder
4 teaspoons onion powder
4 teaspoons chili powder

2 teaspoons coriander
2 teaspoons cumin
2 teaspoons Italian herbs
1 teaspoon oregano
1 teaspoon black pepper
1 teaspoon salt

Preparation time: 10 minutes. Combine all ingredients in a mixer and blend thoroughly. Serve with grilled trout, chicken or rib eye steak.
Yield: 1 pound, serves 20 people.

If you desire a little more heat from the butter, add more cayenne and chili powder.

Serve with Inglenook-Napa Valley Estate Bottled Zinfandel.

Jamie Morningstar
for
Inglenook-Napa Valley

Santa Fe Style Salsa

40 tomatillos
2 bunches cilantro, medium chop
1 medium onion, finely chopped
4 seranno chilies, thinly chopped
with seeds

5 jalapenos, quarter, remove
  seeds and chop fine
2 tablespoons ground cumin
Juice from 1 lime
2 cloves garlic, crushed
Salt and pepper to taste

Soak tomatillos in warm water for 5 minutes, remove husks, and boil until tender (about 10 minutes). Drain excess water. Blend or puree tomatillos, and add the rest of the above ingredients.

Serve as an accompaniment to grilled meats and Eberle Cabernet Sauvignon.
Serves 8 to 10.

Chef Robert Goodfriend, Santa Fe, New Mexico
for
Eberle Winery

Cranberry Salsa

1 12-ounce bag cranberries (frozen can be used)
2-3 cloves of garlic
1-2 jalapeno chilies
4 tablespoons finely chopped cilantro

3 green onions, minced
1/3 cup lime juice (approximately 3 limes)
1/2 cup sugar
Salt and pepper to taste

Boil cranberries in 1 quart of water for 1 minute. Drain well. Mince garlic, then seed and mince jalapenos. Combine with the cilantro, scallions, and cranberries in a mixing bowl. Hand mix, add lime juice, sugar, and salt and pepper.

A great change of pace from traditional cranberry sauce with turkey!

Serve with Lambert Brioge Zinfandel or Nouveau Beaujolais.

Julia Iantosca, Winemaker
Lambert Bridge

Jack London Zinfandel Peppercorn Sauce

1/4 cup mixed whole peppercorns
1/4 cup Zinfandel
1 tablespoon sweet-hot mustard

1 tablespoon balsamic vinegar
1/2 cup extra virgin olive oil

Grind 1/4 cup peppercorns in spice grinder, or use a mortar and pestle. Bring 1/4 cup Zinfandel to a slight boil. Lower heat and simmer until wine is reduced to 1 tablespoon. Blend peppercorns, mustard, vinegar and reduced Zinfandel in a food processor. Add olive oil slowly while processor is on. Continue blending after adding oil until sauce is thickened, about 1 to 2 minutes. Sauce will separate if it gets too warm! Refrigerate until ready to use.   Makes 1/2 cup.

Carlo DiClemente, Winery Chef
Kenwood Vineyards

Blackberry-Mint Butter

Preparation Time: 5 minutes

2 cups fresh or frozen blackberries (if frozen, drain off excess liquid)
1/4 cup fresh chopped mint
1/2 pound sweet butter at room temperature

Combine all ingredients in a food processor and pulse a few times to get mixture going. Then, just let the machine run until all ingredients are well mixed together. Butter will be a rich, dark purple color.

Yields 1/2 pound, serves 10 people.

Walnut-Mustard Butter

Preparation Time: 5 minutes

1 1/2 cups walnuts
1/4 cup whole grain mustard
1/2 pound sweet butter at room temperature
Salt and pepper to taste

Follow the same procedures for the Blackberry-Mint Butter recipe above. This time, the butter will be light brown in color.

Yields 1/2 pound, serves 10 people.

Serve either or both of these butters with grilled New York steak, salmon, chicken or anything else that you may want to try.

Serve with Inglenook-Napa Valley, Estate Bottled, Reserve Pinot Noir.

Jamie Morningstar
for
Inglenook-Napa Valley

Minted Red Onion-Blackberry Relish

Serve with unseasoned beef, grilled, sauteed or broiled.

4 tablespoons olive oil
8 cups red onions, thinly sliced (4 large or 6 medium onions)
1 cup blackberries (Fresh or frozen. May substitute unsweetened raspberries.)

2 teaspoons fresh mint, finely chopped
1/2 teaspoon black pepper, finely ground

In olive oil, saute onions over low heat until coated with oil. Cover pan and cook slowly, stirring frequently, until onions are soft and translucent. Add blackberries and cook, mashing them slightly until fruit is well blended. Add mint and black pepper and stir briefly to blend flavors.   Makes 2 cups, serves 8.

This recipe was developed for Kendall-Jackson's Vintner's Reserve Zinfandel. This wine is bursting with fresh raspberry and blackberry flavors and spiced with a liberal amount of black pepper. The berries and freshly ground pepper in this dish emphasize these qualities.

Kendall-Jackson Vineyard

Mint

Pearl Onion Compote

2 pounds pearl onions, peeled
4 ounces dry raisins
4 ounces peanut oil
3 ounces wine vinegar
3 ounces tomato paste
6 cloves garlic, peeled, crushed

2 sprigs each parsley and
  fresh thyme
6 leaves of sage
2 bay leaves
Chardonnay to cover
Salt and pepper as necessary

Combine all ingredients in a stainless steel pot. Bring to simmer over low heat. Cover. Simmer until tender. Cool.

Serve room temperature as a salad on a bed of young greens, as a garnish to a duck or pheasant terrine, or as part of a "Hors d'Oeuvre" plate.

Note: If compote is too runny, strain and cook liquid slowly until syrupy, combine with onions and chill. Six servings as salad. Eight to ten servings as garnish.

Chef Jean-Paul Weber
Chez Paul Restaurant, Chicago
for
J. Lohr Winery

Dried Fruit Chutney

1 pound dried apricots, chopped
1 cup raisins
1 cup dried papaya, pineapple or
other sweet dried fruit, chopped
1/2 pound preserved ginger,
chopped
2 cups diced onions
2 1/2 cups cider vinegar

2 1/2 cups dark brown sugar
1 tablespoon salt
1 tablespoon dry mustard
1 teaspoon cayenne
1/2 teaspoon turmeric
Grated rind and juice of 1
orange

Combine all the ingredients together in a large non-reactive pot and bring to a boil. Reduce the flame to keep at a simmer until the chutney has thickened. Stir occasionally to prevent scorching. That's it. Makes 3 1/2 cups.

Chefs Robert Engel and Christine Topolos
Russian River Vineyards Restaurant

A sharp, hot chutney that is very easy to make. This condiment will add zest when served with beef, veal, chicken or turkey.

Brandied Cranberry Apple Relish

4 tart apples, peeled and diced
2 pounds fresh cranberries
2 cups sugar
1 cup golden raisins
1 cup orange juice
1 medium onion, chopped fine

2 tablespoons grated orange
rind
2 teaspoons cinnamon
1/2 teaspoon nutmeg
1/2 cup good Brandy

Mix together all ingredients in a sauce pan, except Brandy.

Bring to boil, then reduce heat and simmer slowly for 45 minutes, watching so it will not stick. Cook until thick. Stir in Brandy. Remove from heat. Cool.

This relish is especially good with poultry or pork.

Landmark Vineyards

Apple Chutney

5 medium apples, cored and
  chopped fine (about 7 cups)
2 cups brown sugar
1 3/4 cups cider vinegar

3 to 5 slices of ginger, each
  the size of a quarter
1/4 teaspoon white pepper
1/4 teaspoon ground mace
1/8 teaspoon ground clove

Bring all the above to a boil together, then reduce to a simmer. Stir occasionally and continue cooking over low heat until the apples are very soft and the liquid is almost completely evaporated and absorbed.

Remove the ginger slices and chill before serving.

I like crisp Rome apples or Pippins for chutney and I don't bother peeling them. You don't have to peel the ginger either, since the slices are removed before serving.   Makes about 3 1/2 cups.

Chefs Robert Engel and Christine Topolos
Russian River Vineyards Restaurant

Chutney is a sweet and sour condiment, usually fruit based. This is a very simple, easy to make recipe.

Herbed and Spiced Butters

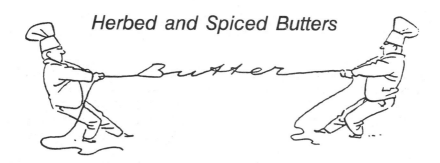

There is, probably, no easier way to transform an ordinary dish into something truly special, than by whipping up an herbed or spiced butter to serve with it.

Your basic measurement is one half cup of butter, softened or melted, to which you add the herbs and/or spices as specified. Don't heat the butter and the herbs and spices together -- add them to the butter after it is softened or melted.

BASIL BUTTER
1 teaspoon basil
1 1/2 teaspoons grated onion

Hamburgers, Italian green beans

CHILI BUTTER
1/2 teaspoon basil leaves, crumbled
1 teaspoon chili powder

Hot corn, tomatoes, chicken, frankfurters, fish

CHIVE BUTTER
1/16 teaspoon ground black pepper
1 1/2 tablespoons freeze dried chives
Lemon juice to taste
Salt to taste

Cabbage, carrots, potatoes, corn, green beans, peas, fish, chicken, liver, mushrooms, grilled meats, oysters, turnips, ham or egg salad sandwiches

CURRY BUTTER
1 teaspoon curry powder
Dusting of ground black pepper and paprika

Potatoes, spinach, cauliflower, corn, chicken, fish, lima beans

DILL BUTTER
1 teaspoon dill weed

Mushrooms, potatoes, carrots, beans, asparagus, spinach, zucchini, fish, chicken, veal

GARLIC BUTTER
1 teaspoon minced fresh garlic

Fish, pasta, bread, grilled meats, spinach, zucchini, cabbage, lima beans

HERBED BUTTER
1 teaspoon powdered mustard
1/8 cup parsley
1 tablespoon fresh shallots
1/2 teaspoon tarragon leaves

Grilled meats, poultry, fish, peas, carrots, celery, green beans

MUSTARD BUTTER
1 1/2 teaspoons powdered mustard

Ham, pork, cauliflower, broiled salmon and seafood, lentils, lima beans, eggs, greens, sandwiches

NUTMEG BUTTER
1 teaspoon ground nutmeg

Shrimp and seafood, spinach, snap beans, broccoli, brussels sprouts, squash, sweet potatoes, carrots, corn, broiled chicken, peas

PARSLEY BUTTER
1/2 teaspoon crushed parsley flakes

Omelets, clams, white fish, potatoes, carrots, mushrooms, parsnips, corn bread, snails

THYME BUTTER
1/2 teaspoon thyme leaves

Fish, chicken, mushrooms, carrots, broiled tomatoes

Desserts

SPICES OF THE WORLD

Baked Peach with Warm Raspberry Compote

HAZELNUT MIXTURE:

1 cup ground hazelnuts
1/4 cup cream cheese
1 tablespoon sour cream
1/2 teaspoon cinnamon
1/4 teaspoon allspice
1 large egg
Sugar to taste

RASPBERRY COMPOTE:

4 pints fresh raspberries
2 tablespoons unsalted butter
1 tablespoon lemon zest
1/2 cup Semillon
2 tablespoons sugar

3 ripe peaches
1 cup Semillon

PREPARE HAZELNUT MIXTURE:

Place hazelnuts in a food processor and grind. Add cream cheese and sour cream. Mix well and add spices. Add egg and sugar to taste. Reserve.

PREPARE RASPBERRY COMPOTE:

Saute berries in butter. Add wine and sugar and bring to a boil. Add zest.

PREPARE PEACHES:

Cut peaches in half, remove pit and hollow out slightly. Fill with hazelnut mixture and bake, covered, for 30 minutes.

TO FINISH:

Remove peaches from oven. Pour raspberry sauce onto each plate and place peach on top. Just before serving, drizzle over a splash of Semillon. Garnish with fresh mint and flowers. Serve warm. Serves 6.

Enjoy with Vichon Botrytis Semillon.

Holly Peterson, Head Chef
Wine and Food Education Department
Robert Mondavi Winery

Late Harvest Apple Cake

1 cup golden raisins
1/2 cup late harvest
 Gewurztraminer or Riesling
2 3/4 cups flour
1 1/2 teaspoons baking soda
1 1/2 teaspoons cinnamon
1/2 teaspoon baking powder
1/2 teaspoon salt
1/2 teaspoon nutmeg

1/4 teaspoon allspice
1/4 teaspoon ginger
3/4 cup sweet butter, room
 temperature
1 3/4 cups sugar
3 large or 4 medium eggs,
 beaten
1 3/4 cups unsweetened
 applesauce

Soak raisins in gently boiling late harvest wine for 10 minutes. Mix all dry ingredients. Beat butter and sugar together. In alternating fashion, add eggs and flour mixture to butter mixture. Fold in raisins and applesauce. Pour into buttered and floured bundt pan. Bake at 350 degrees for 1 hour or until done.

Recommended wine: Chateau St. Jean Johannisberg Riesling, Russian River Valley.

Linda Hagen, Executive Chef
for
Chateau St. Jean

Chocolate Pumpkin Cake

Fine dry bread crumbs
2 3/4 cups flour
3/4 cup unsweetened cocoa
2 teaspoons baking powder
1 teaspoon baking soda
1 1/2 teaspoons cinnamon
1/2 teaspoon each ginger and slat
1/4 teaspoon each cloves and
 nutmeg
1 cup softened butter or margarine

2 cups granulated sugar
1 1/2 teaspoons vanilla
4 eggs
1 can (1 pound) pumpkin (1
 3/4 cups)
1 1/2 cups coarsely chopped
 pecans
Confectioners sugar

Thoroughly grease a 3-quart fluted tube pan. Sprinkle with bread crumbs. Set aside.

Mix well flour, cocoa, baking powder, baking soda, cinnamon, ginger, slat, cloves and nutmeg. Set aside. In large bowl, cream butter with granulated sugar and vanilla. Add eggs, one at a time, beating well after each. Stir in half the flour mixture, then the pumpkin, then remaining flour mixture just until well blended. Stir in walnuts.

Turn batter into pan and smooth top. Bake in a 325 degree oven for 80 to 90 minutes, or until pick inserted in middle of cake comes out clean. Remove from oven; let stand on rack 15 minutes. Invert on rack and cool completely. Remove pan, cover and let stand several hours or overnight before serving. Dust with confectioners sugar or frost with your favorite chocolate frosting.   Serves 10 to 12.

Chocolate and spices ... great! VMH

Carneros Brandied Fruit Cake

1 cup Brandy
1 1/2 cups butter
2 1/2 cups brown sugar
1 tablespoon cinnamon
1/2 tablespoon allspice
1/2 tablespoon nutmeg
1/2 tablespoon clove
5 eggs
1 1/4 cups raspberry or blackberry jam

2 1/2 cups raisins (combine golden and black)
2 1/2 cups chopped dried figs (black mission)
5 cups unbleached white flour, sifted together with 1 tablespoon baking soda
2 1/2 cups toasted and chopped walnuts or pecans

Soak the raisins and figs in the Brandy for at least 2 hours. Cream butter, then add brown sugar and spices. Cream until light. Add eggs, beating after each addition. Stir in jam. Transfer to a large mixing bowl. Add dry ingredients. Fold in toasted chopped nuts and soaked raisins and figs. Pour into prepared loaf pans (buttered and floured). Bake in a preheated oven at 325 degrees for 40 minutes to 1 hour. While still warm, brush each cake liberally on all sides with Brandy.

When cool, wrap in plastic wrap or parchment paper and keep in a tightly closed tin.

If you wish to age the cakes, they may be periodically brushed with more Brandy. The cakes can be made as early as September, to be served at Christmas time. Makes 4 large loaves.

Michelle Mutrux
for
Carneros Alambic Distillery

Caramel Lavender Ice Cream

1 cup heavy cream
2 cups regular milk
2/3 cup sugar
3/4 cup honey
6 egg yolks

Seeds scraped from 1 vanilla
 bean
Flowers and buds from 1
 sprig of lavender

Cream egg yolks and sugar until thick and ribbon-like. Add seeds from vanilla bean to egg/sugar mixture. Bring heavy cream, milk and lavender to boil. Very slowly, strain milk into egg mixture while continuously beating. In heavy sauce pan, caramelize honey until rich amber in color. Put milk and egg mixture in another heavy sauce pan, turn on heat to low, and slowly add caramelized honey, whisking continuously. Cool in refrigerator 1 1/2 to 2 hours, then freeze in ice cream maker according to manufacturer's directions.

Makes about 1 1/2 quarts.

Sarah Kaswan, Chef
Matanzas Creek Winery

Chocolate Lavender Truffles

12 ounces bittersweet chocolate,
 finely chopped
1 cup heavy cream

2 tablespoons Grand Marnier
Flowers and buds from 1
 sprig of Lavender

Bring heavy cream and lavender to boil. Boil 1 minute and strain over chopped chocolate in bowl. Add Grand Marnier and stir occasionally until chocolate is completely melted. Cool in refrigerator 3 hours until completely set. With warm spoon, roll truffle mixture into small balls (cherry size). Then roll truffles in sifted unsweetened cocoa or dip in melted chocolate. Yum!

Delicious with Matanzas Creek Merlot.

Sarah Kaswan, Chef
Matanzas Creek Winery

Lemon Curd Tart with Hazelnut Crust and Fresh Local Fruit

PASTRY INGREDIENTS:

4 ounces butter, unsalted
1 cup all purpose flour
3 tablespoons granulated sugar
2 tablespoons darkly toasted fresh
 hazelnuts, finely chopped

Pinch of salt
Ice water (as needed)

PREPARE PASTRY:

Combine dry ingredients in large mixing bowl. Cut cold butter into small cubes, then add to dry ingredients and blend with a fork until thoroughly mixed and forms a solid mass. Add ice water to the pastry as needed. Allow pastry to rest, chilled for at least 30 minutes. Butter tart pan, dust with flour, then chill. Roll out pastry and form a thin tart crust inside baking dish. Cut away excess pastry. Bake in a 375 degree oven for 15 to 20 minutes or until lightly golden brown. Remove from oven and cool to room temperature.

LEMON CURD INGREDIENTS:

2 large lemons (peel and juice)
1/2 cup butter, unsalted

1 cup superfine sugar
3 eggs, lightly beaten

PREPARE LEMON CURD:

Remove zest from lemons with a peeler, then slice as thin as possible. Squeeze juice from lemons. Melt butter in saucepan over medium flame and gradually stir in the sugar. Add beaten eggs, lemon juice and zest and continue cooking. Stir until thickened, then remove from heat and cool.

FRUITS AND GARNISHES:

2-3 small ripe mangos
1 pint basket strawberries
1 pint basket raspberries
1/4 cup lemon zest (from 2-3
lemons)

1/2 cup pistachios
6 nasturtium blossoms and
 leaves
Powdered sugar, for dusting

PREPARE FRUIT:

Peel mangoes and cut off the two sides from the pit. Thinly slice the mangoes lengthwise. Rinse strawberries and remove stems. Cut strawberries in half. Remove zest from 2 to 3 lemons with a peeler and slice as thin as possible. Coarsely chop pistachios. Pluck nasturtium blossoms and leaves for garnishing.

ASSEMBLE TART:

Evenly spread the lemon curd halfway inside the tart shell. Decoratively arrange the mangoes, strawberries and raspberries on top of the lemon curd. Sprinkle the tart with half of the chopped pistachios.

TO SERVE:

Dust the tart lightly with powdered sugar. Slice the tart in six equal pieces and place a slice on each plate. Sprinkle lemon zest and chopped pistachios lightly onto each plate and garnish with nasturtium blossoms and leaves.   Serves 6.

Enjoy with Robert Mondavi Moscato D'Oro

Holly Peterson, Head Chef
Wine and Food Education Department
Robert Mondavi Winery

Fresh Thyme and Tomato Sherbet

24 medium-size tomatoes
4 1/2 cups fresh or canned tomato
 juice
1/8 teaspoon cayenne pepper
8 sprigs fresh thyme
1 teaspoon chopped fresh thyme
Juice of 1/2 lemon, strained

6 ounces sugar
7 ounces water
2 ounces glucose (heavy
 white corn syrup)
Salt and freshly ground
 pepper to taste

To make the syrup, combine sugar, water and glucose in a sauce pan and bring to a boil, stirring occasionally. Boil for 3 minutes, skimming the surface of any white foam that may appear. Strain and set aside to cool.

Blanch the tomatoes by putting them into a sauce pan of boiling, salted water for 10 seconds and them immediately into cold water to stop them from cooking further. Skin them, cut 1/3 off the stem end of the tomato and a thin slice off the other end so it will stand firmly. Remove the seeds and cores, season the inside with salt and freshly ground pepper. Place upside down on a plate in the refrigerator.

In a bowl, mix well the tomato juice, lemon juice, syrup, chopped thyme and cayenne pepper with the salt and freshly ground black pepper (if the mixture is still a little too acidic, add a little more salt to balance it).

Pour mix into an ice cream machine and churn for 10 to 20 minutes. This will vary depending on the machine. The sherbet should be smooth and velvety. Fill the finished sherbet into the tomato shells. Place 3 per person onto a chilled plate and decorate with thyme sprigs. If available, use Sun Gold or Sweet Million cherry tomatoes for a garnish as well. Serves 8.

Serve with Chateau Souverain Gewurztraminer.

**Martin W. Courtman, Executive Chef
Chateau Souverain**

Cinnamon Chocolate Pecan Pie

One 9-inch pie crust

FILLING:

1 cup light corn syrup	1 teaspoon cinnamon
1/2 cup sugar	3 eggs
1/4 cup margarine or butter, melted	1 (6-ounce) package (1 cup) semi-sweet chocolate chips
1 teaspoon vanilla	1 1/2 cups pecan halves

TOPPING:

Whipped cream	1 teaspoon powdered sugar
1/2 teaspoon cinnamon	

Prepare pie crust according to package directions for filled on-crust pie, using 9-inch pie pan. Hat oven to 325 degrees.

In a large bowl, combine corn syrup, sugar, margarine, vanilla, cinnamon and eggs and beat well. Stir in chocolate chips and 1 1/2 cups pecans. Spread evenly in pie crust-lined pan. Bake at 325 degrees for 55 to 65 minutes or until deep golden brown and filling is set. Cover edge of pie crust with strip of foil after 15 to 20 minutes of baking to prevent excessive browning. Cool completely.

Garnish pie with whipped cream to which you have added cinnamon and powdered sugar. Refrigerate. Serves 8.

Do not plan on any leftovers! VMH

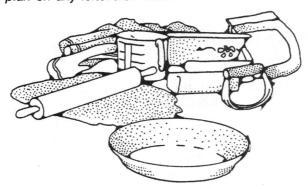

Persimmon Walnut Cake with Champagne Sea Foam Sauce

1 1/2 cups walnuts, coarsely chopped
1 1/2 cups bittersweet chocolate, chunks (or chocolate chips)
3 cups flour
3 teaspoons baking powder
1 teaspoon ground cinnamon
1 teaspoon ground ginger (or 1 tablespoon minced candied ginger)
1/2 teaspoon freshly grated nutmeg
1 cup sweet butter, softened (2 sticks)
2 cups sugar
1 1/2 cups persimmon pureé (or pumpkin)
4 eggs
3/4 cup Blanc de Noirs Champagne

Toss the nuts and chocolate in 1/2 cup of the flour. Sift the remaining dry ingredients together. Set aside. Cream the butter and sugar in a mixing bowl until fluffy. Beat in the pureé and then the eggs, one at a time. Fold in the dry ingredients, alternately with the champagne. Stir in the nuts and chocolate. Pour the batter into an ungreased 10 tube or bundt pan. Bake 1 hour and 15 minutes at 325 degrees. Cool and remove from the pan.

Serve in slices with Sea Foam Sauce or whipped cream. Serves 12.

CHAMPAGNE SEA FOAM SAUCE:

2 tablespoons butter, softened
2 tablespoons flour
1/2 cup sugar
1 egg, separated
1/2 cup Blanc de Noirs Champagne
1 teaspoon vanilla

Whisk together the butter, flour and sugar in a saucepan. Beat the egg yolk into the champagne, and stir into the butter mixture. Cook over low heat, stirring constantly, until thickened. Cool. Just before serving, add the vanilla, and fold in the beaten egg white. Makes 1 1/2 cups.

Serve with Korbel Champagne/Blanc de Noirs

Teresa Douglas/Mitchell, Culinary Director
Korbel Champagne Cellars

Ricotta Cheese-Lemon Thyme Tart
with Sweet Cornmeal Crust

CORNMEAL CRUST:

1/2 cup butter, at room
 temperature
1/4 cup sugar
1 cup yellow cornmeal

2 eggs, at room temperature
1 teaspoon salt
1 1/2 cups all-purpose flour

Beat butter and sugar until smooth. Add cornmeal, eggs, and salt, and beat until well combined. Add flour and mix until dough forms a ball. Mixture should be soft and moist. Wrap in plastic and chill for 1 hour. Roll out the crust to fit a prepared 9-inch by 1-inch tart pan with removable bottom. Wrap and save any leftover dough in freezer. Prick with a fork several times and bake for 8 minutes at 350 degrees until just lightly brown. (Leftover dough is good for making biscuits.)

RICOTTA CHEESE-LEMON THYME FILLING:

4 tablespoons minced shallot or
 green onion
1 tablespoon butter
2/3 cup heavy cream
1/2 cup Fumé Blanc
1/2 teaspoon salt
1/4 teaspoon ground white pepper

12 ounces fresh ricotta cheese
3 eggs
1 1/2 tablespoons chopped
 fresh lemon thyme or other
 fresh herbs (chives, parsley,
 basil)

Saute shallots in butter until soft, not brown. Add cream, wine, salt and white pepper. Reduce by one half. Cool. Add ricotta cheese, eggs and thyme and beat until smooth. Pour into the prepared tart shell.

Bake in a 350 degree oven for 35 to 40 minutes, or until filling is just set and lightly browned. Serve warm, or at room temperature. Garnish with sprinkling of edible flowers.

Recommended wine: Fetzer Valley Oaks Fumé Blanc. The crisp, distinctively herbaceous flavors of the wine play a perfect counterpart to the tart.

Chef John Ash, Culinary Director
Fetzer Vineyards

Poached Pears in Zinfandel

4 ripe, but firm Comice, Bartlett or
  Bosc pears
3 cups Zinfandel
1 1/2 cups sugar
Zest and juice of 1 lemon
1/4 of a cinnamon stick

1 vanilla bean, split in half
  lengthwise
2 peppercorns
1 clove
1 thyme sprig
4 mint sprigs

Mix the Zinfandel, sugar, vanilla bean, spices, herbs and lemon zest in a sauce pan, bring to a boil and simmer for 5 minutes. Carefully peel, core and cut the pears in half. Dip each half in the lemon juice before immediately immersing it in the simmering syrup. Simmer for 8 to 10 minutes, or until a small knife inserted in the middle of the pear meets a slight resistance. Carefully pour everything into a bowl, letting it cool (several hours will do, but overnight is best).

Take out two halves at a time. Starting at the bottom of each pear, slice them 3/4 of the way up (lengthwise), enabling you to fan out the halves. Place the two uncut tops of the pears together, strain a little of the syrup over them and garnish with a mint sprig.   Serves 4.

Serve with delicate French cookies on the side.

**Martin W. Courtman, Executive Chef
Chateau Souverain**

Pear Gingerbread Upside Down Cake

3 pears, peeled and halved
2 tablespoons butter
2 tablespoons brown sugar

Melt butter with brown sugar and put in the bottom of a square 9-inch by 9-inch pan, along with the pears cut side down.

1/3 cup butter	1 teaspoon cinnamon
1/3 cup sugar	1 teaspoon ground ginger
1 egg	1/4 teaspoon ground cloves
1/2 cup molasses	1/2 teaspoon salt
1 1/2 cups flour	1/2 cup hot water
3/4 teaspoon baking soda	

Mix all of the above ingredients together. Pour batter over pears and bake 50 minutes at 350 degrees. Cool 10 minutes and invert onto serving platter.

Serve with De Loach Vineyards Late Harvest Gewurztraminer.

Christine De Loach
De Loach Vineyards

Brandied Bananas

3 ripe but firm bananas	1/4 cup grated coconut
1/2 cup orange juice	3 tablespoons butter or
1/2 cup Brandy	margarine
1/4 cup brown sugar	1/2 cup whipping cream
1/2 teaspoon cinnamon	

Peel bananas, slice lengthwise, and arrange cut side down in glass baking plate. Cover with sauce of orange juice, mixed with the brandy. Sprinkle brown sugar, cinnamon, and grated coconut and dot with butter. Bake in moderate oven for 20 minutes. Serve with whipped cream. Serves 6.

Conn Creek Winery

Ginger Pear Tarte

CRUST:

8 tablespoons sweet butter, chilled
1 cup flour
1 tablespoon sugar

3-4 drops almond extract
1 tablespoon water

Mix ingredients with pastry blender or finger tips, mixing uniformly. Roll into circle approximately 1 1/2 inches larger than tart pan (9 to 10 inch pan). Bake at 425 degrees for 10 minutes.

FILLING:

1/2 cup sugar
4 tablespoons flour
2 eggs
2 tablespoons candied ginger
 chopped

1/2 cup melted unsalted butter
3 pears peeled, cored and
 sliced into fan shape (can
 use apples or seedless
 grapes)

Combine sugar, flour, eggs and ginger. Slowly whisk in melted butter. Arrange pears in crust, pour filling mixture around pears. Bake at 375 degrees for 1 hour, until golden.

Linda Hagen, Executive Chef
Chateau St. Jean

Chocolate Bread Pudding

2 eggs
1 1/2 cups fine, soft bread crumbs
3 cups milk, scalded
1 tablespoon butter
1/2 cup semi-sweet chocolate
chips

3 squares unsweetened
 chocolate, melted
2/3 cup sugar
1/4 teaspoon salt
1 teaspoon vanilla
1 teaspoon cinnamon

Beat eggs, add bread crumbs, milk, butter, sugar, cinnamon and salt.
Mix well. Add melted chocolate and vanilla, folding in chocolate chips.
Pour into a greased baking dish and bake in a moderate oven, 325
degrees, until firm. Serve hot or cold with whipped cream.

*This recipe is from my own family cookbook, now in its third generation.
I updated it by adding chocolate chips and cinnamon. The results?
Judge for yourself. VMH.*

Spicy Chocolate Macaroons

1 1/2 cups coconut flakes
1/2 cup sugar
2 squares unsweetened chocolate,
 melted
3 tablespoons flour

1/8 teaspoon salt
1 teaspoon cinnamon
1/2 teaspoon nutmeg
1 teaspoon vanilla
2 egg whites

Combine coconut, sugar, flour, salt, cinnamon and nutmeg in a bowl
and mix. Stir in chocolate, egg whites and vanilla. Mix well.

Drop from teaspoon on lightly greased baking sheets.

Bake at 325 degrees for 20 to 25 minutes, or until edges brown.
Remove from baking sheets.   Makes about 18 to 20.

Better double this recipe, these are really, really good. VMH

Biscotti

6 eggs
2 cups sugar
3 cups sifted flour
3 teaspoons baking powder
Grated lemon rind
1 1/2 cubes melted butter
1 teaspoon vanilla

2 teaspoons almond extract
1 teaspoon (or more) anise seed
1 teaspoon anise extract
1 jigger Brandy
1 cup chopped almonds

Cream together eggs, sugar, flour and baking powder. Add the rest of the ingredients. Pour onto greased cookie sheet with edges. Bake at 350 degrees for 30 to 40 minutes. Cut into serving-size biscuits and place each piece on its side on cookie sheet. The biscotti will not all fit on one cookie sheet. Return to oven for a few minutes to brown slowly so they are nice and crunchy. Don't forget to toast both sides.

Perfect for dunking into Sausal Zinfandel or Cabernet.

**Roselee Demonstene & Cindy Martin, Co-Owners
Sausal Winery**

This recipe for Biscotti Cookies also appeared in our two previous California Wine Country Cookbooks, and is included in this book because of the response it received. VMH.

Spicy Peppernut Cookies

1 cup brown sugar, packed
4 tablespoons butter, softened
1 egg
1 teaspoon brandy
1 3/4 cups flour

1/4 teaspoon baking soda
1/4 teaspoon cloves
1/4 teaspoon ginger
1/4 teaspoon cinnamon
1/4 teaspoon pepper

Cream butter and brown sugar. Stir in egg and brandy. Mix dry ingredients and add, mixing with hands. Shape into balls and place 1 inch apart on baking sheet. Bake in 375 degree oven for 8 minutes or until lightly browned. Keep covered tightly in tin or store in deep freeze.   Makes 70.

Serve with Quivira Zinfandel.

Holly P. Wendt, Proprietor
Quivira Vineyards

This recipe, which appeared in our last book, is included as an "extra" in this one because it is so good, and so easy to make. We wanted to include it for your pleasure. VMH.

INDEX

This book, "The California Wine Country Herbs and Spices Cookbook" is the third in the series.

The second, "The California Wine Country Cookbook II," and the first, "The California Wine Country Cookbook" are also available.

Each are $15.95, which includes shipping and handling.

A full-color, 5 X 7-inch print of the illustration on the cover of this book, suitable for framing, is $15.95 including shipping and handling.

Send your personal check or money order to: The Hoffman Press, P.O. Box 2996, Santa Rosa, CA 95405. Your money back if you are not delighted.